THE ESSENTIAL POETS

THE ESSENTIAL
POE

Edgar Allan Poe

BORN 19 JANUARY 1809
DIED 7 OCTOBER 1849

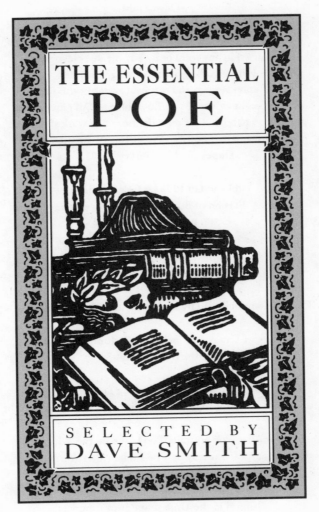

THE ESSENTIAL
POE

SELECTED BY
DAVE SMITH

GALAHAD BOOKS
NEW YORK

Published in 1993 by Galahad Books
A division of Budget Book Service, Inc.
386 Park Avenue South
New York, NY 10016
Galahad Books is a registered trademark
of Budget Book Service, Inc.

This edition published by arrangement with The Ecco Press

Library of Congress Catalog Card Number: 90-43745
ISBN: 0-88365-834-8

Original design by Reg Perry
Additional art and design for this edition by Cindy LaBreacht

Edgar Allan Poe portrait "Poe based on the Whitman
daguerreotype" courtesy of The Edgar Allan Poe Museum,
The Poe Foundation, Inc., Richmond Virginia.

Printed in the United States of America.

 CONTENTS

To Mary Alice Cornwell
—source of dreams
&
to C. Edward Russell, Jr.
—hunter and friend

THE ESSENTIAL
POE

# INTRODUCTION

On October 9, 1849, in the New York *Tribune*, "Ludwig," the pseudonym of the Reverend Rufus Wilmot Griswold, announced that "Edgar Allan Poe is dead."

> He died in Baltimore the day before yesterday. This will startle many but few will be grieved by it. The poet was well-known personally or by reputation, in all this country; he has readers in England, and in several of the states of Continental Europe; but he had few or no friends.

Poe the writer, as Griswold suggested, had become a literary star, perhaps America's first. His reputation today is blacker because Griswold's obituary and subsequent accusations emphasized Poe as a decadent, a misfit, and an outlaw. This image of Poe, reinforced by ill-informed biographies, literary paparazzi, and cheap horror movies, has also made Poe the most mysterious of American poets. His public appeal and his reputation as a writer (although not as a poet) may actually be greater now than ever.

Edgar Poe was born January 19, 1809, in Boston to David and Elizabeth Poe, both actors. Poe's mother, then 22, was English. Within a year, David Poe, a native of Baltimore, vanished. By the fall of 1811, Mrs. Poe's performing engagements up and down the east coast left her, at last, in Richmond, Virginia, with her three children, William Henry, Rosalie, and Edgar.

For Elizabeth Poe, the nomadic theater life meant seasons on the road, poverty, no stable home for her children, and a good chance of an early

death. When tuberculosis killed her on December 8, 1811, Richmond merchant John Allan and his wife, Frances, took Edgar Poe, not yet three, as their foster son. He thereby narrowly escaped the usual life of the nineteenth century orphan which, as the novels of Charles Dickens recorded, was all too frequently grim and short.

Edgar Poe's chance at a decent life would prove tenuous, but he had at least the early luck of a home, some family, and the sense that he might have potential. An active boy, he boxed and once swam six miles against the James River tide. He was sufficiently prominent to have been made a uniformed lieutenant of ceremonial guards when the Revolutionary War hero the Marquis de Lafayette made a tour of the city in 1824. John Allan, a prosperous exporter, certainly raised Poe as his heir, perhaps encouraging Poe's touchy pride and ambition to be a gentleman. But Poe and Allan fell out. Ignoring Poe, Allan's will recognized only his illegitimate children.

Poe, despite Edward Wagenknecht's contention that the poet's "manner toward women was reverent in the old chivalric style," must have found the women in his life as vulnerable in their support as in their health. Elizabeth Poe, the mother he revered but could not remember, left him only a miniature watercolor of herself. There is no record he received more from Frances Allan than (and it is everything) the gift of love, a position in her family, and an entree to society. In 1829 Frances Allan died of tuberculosis. Shortly afterward, John Allan married his second wife, Louisa Gabriella Patterson, who wanted no foster son. Poe's first "love," Jane Stanard, the mother of a boyhood friend and subject of his poem "To Helen," died mentally deranged when Poe was fifteen. Within two years Poe was engaged to Elmira Royster. Her father, for unknown reasons, intercepted the poet's letters to her, and at seventeen she married another man. While all lyric poetry has its origin in yearning for the absent love, Poe's is especially concerned with women who vanish. Why not? He had lost four of them before his twenty-first birthday.

If one approach to Poe's ever-mysterious life and art is his relationships with women, another has been, historically, Poe's relationship with his foster father. John Allan, naturalized Scot and disciplined businessman, has long and often been portrayed as Poe's nemesis. However, some recent critics, like David Ketterer, have argued that Allan was "a considerate father" who gave Poe affection, financial support, and an unusual education. Whatever the case, the rupture between them came after Allan sent Poe to the University of Virginia.

Thomas Jefferson was justly proud of founding the University of Virginia, but in 1826 his academic village, then only in its second year, was populated by students who often were less scholars than the self-indulgent, undisciplined sons of the plantation aristocracy. At that time, nothing was more important than the public maintenance of one's status as a "gentleman," although this could and often did mean curiously uncivilized behavior. Poe described one fight's loser as "bitten from the shoulder to the elbow—pieces of flesh as large as my hand [gone]. . . ." Each student "gentleman" was expected to maintain a slave servant and a horse. Allan gave Poe insufficient funds to cover his obligations, and Poe chafed. Perhaps more than most caught up in the usual father-son struggles, Poe gambled to meet his needs and lost in excess of $2,000, a huge amount in 1826. Allan paid some, but not all of the debts.

Poe's student days were ordinary and brief. He excelled in some studies, did poorly in others. The evidence suggests he began to drink. He also began to read and write poems with greater intensity. Feeling that Allan had abused him, he left school, puttered for some months in Richmond, and then sailed for Boston in 1827 where he enlisted in the army as Edgar A. Perry. While there he paid a young printer to get out his *Tamerlane and Other Poems*. By 1829, now a sergeant major, he published *Al Aaraaf, Tamerlane, and Minor Poems*. Shortly after, at age twenty, he was bought out of service by none other than John Allan—a conspicuous act of support for a youth called "difficult" by his most ardent partisans.

Rescued from active army duty, Poe went to West Point in 1830 as a cadet. Though he was a mature "soldier student," Poe allowed himself to be court-martialed for accumulated minor offenses, gave no defense (insuring conviction), and left for New York in the cold February of 1831. But cadet Poe had solicited enough subscribers to underwrite another book. *Poems* appeared in New York in 1831. Poe, now orphaned by family, schools, and the army, appeared in Baltimore.

He turned to his Aunt Maria Clemm. A widowed mother, she took him in as a son. In 1836 Poe married her thirteen-year-old daughter, Virginia, his first cousin. Whether or not the marriage was ever consummated, a matter ordinarily of little relevance to a man's art but of some consequence because of the centrality of women to Poe's vision, has been debated for decades. Nonetheless, if Poe did not experience sexual love, he and "Sissy" were undoubtedly devoted to each other. Now having created a family of his own, Poe undertook his life's major work. He was twenty-four years old.

In 1835 Poe became editor of the *Southern Literary Messenger,* commencing a decade of labor as a "magazinist" who wrote, printed, and sold journals. Then the national voice, journals made and lost fortunes. They educated writers like Poe and Whitman. They were the blue collar Harvard and Yale, providing new writers forums for new visions. Editors shifted from one journal to another like contemporary professional athletes shopping contracts, and Poe's editorial perambulations led him up and down the east coast as his parents had done years before, passing through Philadelphia, landing in New York, and, later, making sorties back to Richmond and Baltimore. He was an excellent editor whose critical discourse set the standards for an American audience still looking to England for its models. He always increased sales, but he consistently got himself dismissed. He drank. He carped. How, overworked, underpaid to the point of poverty, short of time and shorter of cash, could he write?

Yet, write he did. He composed the poetry and fiction which would take him in one decade from an unknown to an American icon. In 1838 he published *The Narrative of Arthur Gordon Pym,* and in 1840 his *Tales of the Grotesque and Arabesque.* In 1843 *The Prose Romances of Edgar A. Poe* appeared, followed in 1845 by *Tales* and *The Raven and Other Poems* (bound in one volume). He would publish *Eureka: A Prose Poem,* his last book, in 1848. Yet, for Poe, success was always followed by devastating failure or loss, or both.

Poe's wife Virginia died of tuberculosis in 1847, coughing up blood as had Elizabeth Poe and Frances Allan. During the next two years Poe flirted with marriage to a number of women, including Mrs. Nancy Richmond (who changed her name to "Annie" after he wrote a poem to her), the poet Mrs. Sarah Helen Whitman, to whom Poe proposed in a cemetery, and his early love, now widowed, Mrs. Elmira Royster Shelton. Whether deliberate or not, his pattern was to fall afoul of his intended, somehow to abort the marriage-to-be, and return to Maria Clemm.

In the early fall of 1848, Poe was in Richmond and Norfolk, Virginia, delivering his lectures and reading poems. He wooed and was, perhaps, engaged to marry Mrs. Shelton. He was famous now, but still forced to hustle an income (one critic says he earned only $6,200 in his lifetime). On September 27, he took a Chesapeake Bay steamer to Baltimore where he was engaged to edit the work of a female poet in Philadelphia. Nothing is known of his whereabouts or activities until October the 3rd, when he was found in Baltimore's 4th ward, semi-conscious, and delivered to Washington College Hospital. On Sunday the 7th, he lapsed from a delirious state and died.

Rufus Griswold's obituary initiated the historical image of Poe: the alcoholic social outlaw obsessed with ghoulish delights. Poe, in a ghastly lapse of judgement, apparently made Griswold his literary executor.

Maria Clemm promptly gave Poe's papers to Griswold who, in 1850, published the first full edition of the work, including his "Memoir" of Poe. In this he lied, claiming among other things that Poe was expelled from the University of Virginia, deserted from the army, tried to seduce John Allan's second wife, and that he was a plagiarist. Poe's standing as a journalist and husband disappeared. But the Poe Griswold created proved hypnotic. This visionary victim and alien genius has since cast his shadow over modern fiction, from engendering a genre to privileging new literary theorists. As a poet, Poe has seen critical enthusiasm's ebb and flow but he has never lacked an audience. Despite flaws, and he has many, Poe's may be the first American poetry of significance.

*   *   *

Robert Hass, the contemporary American poet, has written "All the new thinking is about loss." Poe, though usually opposed to such a didactic line, would have agreed. The subjects of Poe's poetry are commonly those of the pastoral tradition: lost love, the art of poetry, the isolation of the self, a vision of an ideal realm. Such subjects are the marks of a youthful, romantic, and lyric imagination. Almost inevitably the theme of his poems, of which he wrote slightly more than 100, is loss.

The idea of *loss,* of course, defines the modern. Poe might have been shocked at Nietzsche's announcement in 1882 of God's death, but he knew himself to be a spiritual man in a world being unbolted by science, that destroyer of the old faith. In "Sonnet—To Science" the force rending umbilical continuity with the past is science allegorized as a woman, and Poe makes her a virtual gargoyle whose "wings are dull realities" and whose purpose is evidently to stop the poet's "wandering / To seek for treasures in the jewelled skies." When Poe echoes the Edenic fall and suggests this creature has separated man from nature, a modern reader nods and understands:

> *Hast thou not dragged Diana from her car?*
> *And driven the Hamadryad from the wood*

> *To seek a shelter in some happier star?*
>   *Hast thou not torn the Naiad from her flood,*
> *The Elfin from the green grass, and from me*
> *The summer dream beneath the tamarind tree?*

For Poe, as for us, science threatens with an absolute death, our "summer dream" of pure life lapsing into nightmarish memory. He knew personally the ache of being orphaned, and his loss became the emblem for the universal erosions of meaning, personality, and supernatural, or mythic, dreams. But Poe was not a modern. His poems typically seek that "shelter in some happier star" and believe in both an ordering God and a mechanical universe. However different from Dickinson, Melville, Whitman, and Emerson, Poe preceded them in searching for answers to loneliness and fear in the emerging myths of self-reliance, nationalism, science, and religion.

Poe's answer was an idiosyncratic compound of neoplatonic idealism and ur-relativity theory by which he meant to justify the ways of art to man. Poe viewed matter as Godly energy radiating constantly away from God's original unity. He wrote in his prose poem *Eureka:*

> *In the Original Unity of the First Thing lies the*
> *Secondary Cause of All Things, with the Germ of*
> *Their Inevitable Annihilation.*

The death of all things, the result of fragmentation and distance from their source, he thought, must inevitably return them to God and purity. The mechanics, principles, and actions of this cosmological idea composed Poe's creation myth.

All creation myths are commonly dichotomous—there / here, then / now, good / bad. Poe's imagines an ideal existence, perhaps actually located on another planet. Our world is corrupt, or unbeautiful. Art's worship, he thought, should embrace that pure, other reality, not this

world of deception. Poems were dreams for opening the mind. Unlike Freud, who confronted life's actual distortions and possibilities by analyzing dreams, Poe valued dreams as escapes from the brutality of living. In his prose tales, this anti-realistic treatment led to complex and original dramatizations of the psyche's life but in the poems the result was often predictable and conventional.

Poe's intentions, as well as his generic tendencies, are obvious in the opening stanza of "To One In Paradise" (1833):

> *Thou wast that all to me, love,*
> *For which my soul did pine—*
> *A green isle in the sea, love,*
> *A fountain and a shrine,*
> *All wreathed with fairy fruits and flowers,*
> *And all the flowers were mine.*

An anonymous swain laments a lady's passage to a heavenly reward. He lives only to name her abundant, symbolic nature (she is more *place* and *idea* than human) in Byronic gestures and ordinary pastoral imagery. If, as Auden remarked, Poe was seldom at his best in his most typical poem, the hymn in praise of the beloved either dead or simply gone, he understood that the erotic combined with death produced the lyric that shook the heart. Poe saw the thrill of beauty could be evoked by harder, darker dreamscapes.

The January 29, 1845 issue of New York's *Evening Mirror* carried Poe's poem "The Raven." Instantly famous, widely reprinted, and endlessly parodied, "The Raven" displays both Poe's genius and conventional poetics. On the face of it, "The Raven" is absurd. Late at night a lover, missing his dead lady, hears a tapping. Finding no one at the door, he opens the window. A raven flutters in, lights on the bust of Pallas, and *the lover* initiates a catechism in which the predator's mnemonic "Nevermore" answers all assertions or questions. Allegorical, yet overtly

refusing a message, with a closure of endlessness ("And the Raven, never flitting, still is sitting, *still* is sitting"), the poem is the pastoral lyric as nightmare mated to stagy melodrama.

When Ralph Waldo Emerson called Poe "the Jingle Man," he voiced what has become a common critical opinion. Yet, if "The Raven" has seemed to many unintentionally funny and bathetic, this spooky dream is one of the essential poems of the Western mind. With "Ulalume" and "The Bells" it composes a triad of Poe's most ambitious, if metrically clattering, verses. It proved so popular at Poe's poetry readings that he wrote an essay, "The Philosophy of Composition," in which he described "The Raven's" composition as if it were an invention with gears. Emphasizing poetic labor instead of inspiration, in essay and poem, he suggested both the beginning of a modernist poetics and an original American poetry.

Poe's nuts and bolts poetics had begun to find expression early in his "Letter to B———" of 1831 and his lectures ("The Poetic Principle," "The Rationale of Verse") show a continuing, if not entirely coherent attempt to refine a vision. The heart of his poetics is, however, "The Philosophy." All poetry, he said, should be lyric, short, and firmly musical. His business was to create an experience of what he elsewhere called "supernal beauty." This beauty, the essence of the cosmic All, must be quasi-divine. And noticeably missing. Necessarily, the poet's tone would be deeply sorrowful. All of this fit nicely with the nineteenth century's increasingly industrial spirit—romantic, isolated, and doomed. Not surprisingly, Poe concluded "the death, then, of a beautiful woman is, unquestionably, the most poetical topic. . . ."

Self-conscious, isolated, and doomed, this was not the poet avuncular Whitman would send over the rooftops in 1855, nor one the ebullient huckster Emerson would greet with ready approval. But it was half of the century's character, the fearful voice speaking in Melville's black abyss and in Dickinson's matter-of-factly buzzing fly. We are as un-

moved by Poe's logic as by his faith, but the controlled hysteria he feels image by image leads to Frost's "Design" and at last to Ted Hughes's *Crow*.

"Everything in Poe is dead," Allen Tate argued. Certainly the women in Poe's poems are invariably ethereal, pure, platonic, and absent. Like "The Raven's" lost Lenore (or Ligea and Ullalume, names Poe thought synonymous with light) they are emblems of life without toil or trouble, existing only as targets of the lamenting consciousness. Poe said this experience of beauty sought an *"indefinite* instead of a *definite* pleasure"* and he understood that pleasure to mimic the divine in his musical praise, be it of places ("The City in the Sea") or of the opposite sex.

Twentieth century readers might easily regard Poe's poetics as a projection of his own psychic problems; his sanitized world, doubtless, reflected the code of a southern gentleman of the nineteenth century in whose romantic idealizing some of us will find unsullied truth and others will find a troubled sexuality. Edgar Poe's poetry, whether read as echoing covert personality dysfunction, exaggerated romantic aesthetics, or the lugubrious nightmares of a rapidly industrializing America, is for contemporary readers often a sentimental, gauzy verse. Yet in such poems as "The Valley of Unrest," "The City in the Sea," "Alone," "The Sleeper," and "A Dream Within a Dream," Poe's portrait of the cosmic orphan snaps into focus a timeless inner song of loss. With him, we ask, "Is *all* that we see or seem / But a dream within a dream?"

Poe regarded exact versification as an imitation of divine music. He praised originality of verse yet, aside from arguable formal innovations in "The Raven" and "The Bells," his poetry is metrically ordinary. Indeed, as Emerson hinted, Poe's ear often was not flexible enough to catch the subtlest of human speech. Still, a distinctive cadence is, early and late, gallopingly present:

At midnight, in the month of June,
I stand beneath the mystic moon.
An opiate vapour, dewy, dim,
Exhales from out her golden rim.
          —"The Sleeper" (1831)

It was many and many a year ago,
  In a kingdom by the sea,
That a maiden there lived whom you may know
  By the name of Annabel Lee;—
And this maiden she lived with no other thought
  Than to love and be loved by me.
          —"Annabel Lee" (1849)

Poe's rhythmic practices supported the indefiniteness of effect he sought. He primarily wrote the gliding and strutting tetrameter and pentameter line of the lyrical ballad, end-stopped and end-rhymed, which he might jam into artificially doubled ("The Raven") or halved lines ("Eldorado"). He favored sonic devices of repetition that created rhythmic momentum, intensity, and emotional weight, and orchestrated, he hoped, an "ethereal" music. He reinforced his music with spatial stanzas that hypnotically scored his page. If his heavy-handed English verse practices prevented him from achieving, as Whitman and Dickinson did, an original poetry whose sound would be commensurate with the soul's hitherto unexpressed American nature, the deliberate end of his insistent cadence was a drowse, a soporific dream of beauty.

But in that sounding dream Poe's longevity will be found. Viewed as engineered machines or drug-like trances, his poems have never gone out of print. He has been translated into all major languages. More than any American except Frost, he may be the poet known to the popular reader. It is not too much to say his yearning for love, a home of utter peace, a place in the sun—all cast against the grinding onward of the industrial explosion of the future—speaks not merely of the American

Dream of infinite possibility, but also of latent, grotesque futility. Poe's vision understood the new world as orphanage and himself as artist among the Philistines. So do we all.

"Mon semblable,—mon frere," Baudelaire said of his brother Poe, beginning the continental reputation that would bring Poe back to America as a major writer. "Our Cousin," Allen Tate said, and even brahmin T. S. Eliot, deriding what he saw as Poe's crude verse, recognized Poe's emphasis upon an art not tied to moral function and located him behind the symbolists, as symbolist tradition stood behind all the main currents of contemporary art. No matter that Robert Louis Stevenson said of Poe in 1899 that "one is glad to think of him as dead," or that Henry James thought Poe appealed to an adolescent taste—Poe, the poet, has not died, quite.

*   *   *

A chronic and episodic abuser of alcohol, a whiner who constantly begged for cash and couldn't keep job, health, or woman? A self-styled gentleman who possessed no family birthright, no dowry, a suspicious education, and scarce claim on his countrymen's good opinion? A manipulative literary politician and pot-boiling hack whose rage led to vituperative critical attacks, litigation, and public fistfights? Was this Edgar Allan Poe? Or was he a man who from birth, and without cessation lifelong, knew in hard fact the poverties of food, cash, shelter, and soul, yet devoted himself to an art whose only end is to achieve permanent delicacy? A man so expressive to the renegade art of the American poet Philip Levine that he would write "My name is Edgar Poe"—is this the man? And who among the selves called Poe is essential? All, I think, are Poe, the first American poet who could not help imagining and limning the nightmare of the entrapped soul. If we feel his poetry sometimes too easily evades the troubled world, we do not fail to know its hunger for freedom or hear its lament for beauty that no loss, no death can diminsh.

In his poem "Alone" Poe wrote: "From childhood's hour I have not been/As others were—I have not seen/As others saw." Yet, as generations of readers have testified, Poe did *see*. In his *Marginalia* he had once advised the poet only to look into his heart and report what was there. He assumed every heart would beat, as his did, to insecurity, loneliness, fear, loss, love, and the answering dream of beauty. His heart's reports came in what, as T. S. Eliot said, "may, in the most nearly literal sense, be called 'the *magic* of verse.' " Nothing Griswold or death or time could do has been able to kill off Edgar Allan Poe. In a few poems and in parts of more than a few poems there is an unforgettable, extraordinarily compelling, and intensely human voice. He may be a dark literary star but he is a star. This is the essential Edgar Allan Poe.

*   *   *

That Poe remains a mystery may be the least of surprises to readers who find that reading Poe and reading about Poe is a labor they often begin but do not end, laying it aside only to return with a curiously renewed interest months and even years later. Among the works concerning Poe on which I have relied are A. H. Quinn's *Edgar Allan Poe, A Critical Biography,* Edward Wagenknecht's *Edgar Allan Poe, The Man Behind the Legend,* Daniel Hoffman's *Poe Poe. Poe Poe Poe Poe Poe,* Julian Symonds' *The Tell-Tale Heart,* and *The Poe Log,* by Dwight Thomas and David K. Jackson. For what poets have thought of Poe, I recommend the introductory essays to various editions of Poe by Allen Tate, W. H. Auden, and Richard Wilbur. For the texts I include here, I have consulted Floyd Stovall's *The Poems of Edgar Allan Poe,* the Library of America's *Poe, Poetry and Tales,* edited by Patrick F. Quinn, and Thomas O. Mabbott's *The Poems of Edgar Allan Poe,* first published in 1969, revised 1980. Mabbott, still the most serviceable, was invaluable to my choices. Many of my notes to the poems are compressions of Mabbott's exhaustive commentaries. No serious reader can ignore him.

—DAVE SMITH

# POEMS

Dreams

Oh! that my young life were a lasting dream!
My spirit not awak'ning till the beam
Of an Eternity should bring the morrow:
Yes! tho' that long dream were of hopeless sorrow,
'Twere better than the dull reality
Of waking life to him whose heart shall be,
And hath been ever, on the chilly earth,
A chaos of deep passion from his birth!

But should it be—that dream eternally
Continuing—as dreams have been to me
In my young boyhood—should it thus be given,
'Twere folly still to hope for higher Heaven!
For I have revell'd, when the sun was bright
In the summer sky; in dreamy fields of light,
And left unheedingly my very heart
In climes of mine imagining—apart
From mine own home, with beings that have been
Of mine own thought—what more could I have seen?

'Twas once and *only* once and the wild hour
From my remembrance shall not pass—some power
Or spell had bound me—'twas the chilly wind
Came o'er me in the night and left behind
Its image on my spirit, or the moon

Shone on my slumbers in her lofty noon
Too coldly—or the stars—howe'er it was
That dream was as that night wind—let it pass.

I have been happy—tho' but in a dream.
I have been happy—and I love the theme—
Dreams! in their vivid colouring of life—
As in that fleeting, shadowy, misty strife
Of semblance with reality which brings
To the delerious eye more lovely things
Of Paradise and Love—and all our own!
Than young Hope in his sunniest hour hath known.

Imitation

A dark unfathom'd tide
Of interminable pride—
A mystery, and a dream,
Should my early life seem;
I say that dream was fraught
With a wild, and waking thought
Of beings that have been,
Which my spirit hath not seen.
Had I let them pass me by,
With a dreaming eye!
Let none of earth inherit
That vision of my spirit;
Those thoughts I would controul,
As a spell upon his soul:
For that bright hope at last
And that light time have past,
And my worldly rest hath gone
With a sigh as it pass'd on:

I care not tho' it perish
With a thought I then did cherish.

The Lake—To————

In spring of youth it was my lot
To haunt of the wide world a spot
The which I could not love the less—
So lovely was the loneliness
Of a wild lake, with black rock bound,
And the tall pines that towered around.

But when the Night had thrown her pall
Upon that spot, as upon all,
And the mystic wind went by
Murmuring in melody—
Then—ah then I would awake
To the terror of the lone lake.

Yet that terror was not fright,
But a tremulous delight—
A feeling not the jewelled mine
Could teach or bribe me to define—
Nor Love—although the Love were thine.

Death was in that poisonous wave,
And in its gulf a fitting grave
For him who thence could solace bring
To his lone imagining—
Whose solitary soul could make
An Eden of that dim lake.

Sonnet—To Science

Science! true daughter of Old Time thou art!
    Who alterest all things with thy peering eyes.
Why preyest thou thus upon the poet's heart,
    Vulture, whose wings are dull realities?
How should he love thee? Or how deem thee wise,
    Who wouldst not leave him in his wandering
To seek for treasure in the jewelled skies,
    Albeit he soared with an undaunted wing?
Hast thou not dragged Diana from her car?
    And driven the Hamadryad from the wood
To seek a shelter in some happier star?
    Hast thou not torn the Naiad from her flood,
The Elfin from the green grass, and from me
The summer dream beneath the tamarind tree?

Romance

Romance, who loves to nod and sing
With drowsy head and folded wing,
Among the green leaves as they shake
Far down within some shadowy lake,
To me a painted paroquet
Hath been—a most familiar bird—
Taught me my alphabet to say—
To lisp my very earliest word
While in the wild wood I did lie,
A child—with a most knowing eye.

Of late, eternal Condor years
So shake the very Heaven on high
With tumult as they thunder by,

I have no time for idle cares
Through gazing on the unquiet sky.
And when an hour with calmer wings
Its down upon my spirit flings—
That little time with lyre and rhyme
To while away—forbidden things!
My heart would feel to be a crime
Unless it trembled with the strings.

To The River Po

Fair river! in thy bright, clear flow
    Of crystal, wandering water,
Thou art an emblem of the glow
    Of beauty—the unhidden heart—
    The playful maziness of art
    In old Alberto's daughter;
But when within thy wave she looks—
    Which glistens then, and trembles—
Why, then the prettiest of brooks
    Her worshipper resembles;
For in his heart, as in thy stream,
    Her image deeply lies—
His heart which trembles at the beam
    Of her soul-searching eyes.

Fairy-Land

Dim vales—and shadowy floods—
And cloudy-looking woods,
Whose forms we can't discover
For the tears that drip all over.

Huge moons there wax and wane—
Again—again—again—
Every moment of the night—
Forever changing places—
And they put out the star-light
With the breath from their pale faces.
About twelve by the moon-dial
One more filmy than the rest
(A kind which, upon trial,
They have found to be the best)
Comes down—still down—and down
With its centre on the crown
Of a mountain's eminence,
While its wide circumference
In easy drapery falls
Over hamlets, over halls,
Wherever they may be—
O'er the strange woods—o'er the sea—
Over spirits on the wing—
Over every drowsy thing—
And buries them up quite
In a labyrinth of light—
And then, how deep!—O, deep!
Is the passion of their sleep.
In the morning they arise,
And their moony covering
Is soaring in the skies,
With the tempests as they toss,
Like—almost any thing—
Or a yellow Albatross.
They use that moon no more
For the same end as before—
Videlicet a tent—
Which I think extravagant:

Its atomies, however,
Into a shower dissever,
Of which those butterflies,
Of Earth, who seek the skies,
And so come down again
(Never-contented things!)
Have brought a specimen
Upon their quivering wings.

Alone

From childhood's hour I have not been
As others were—I have not seen
As others saw—I could not bring
My passions from a common spring—
From the same source I have not taken
My sorrow—I could not awaken
My heart to joy at the same tone—
And all I lov'd—*I* loved alone—
Then—in my childhood—in the dawn
Of a most stormy life—was drawn
From ev'ry depth of good and ill
The mystery which binds me still—
From the torrent, or the fountain—
From the red cliff of the mountain—
From the sun that 'round me roll'd
In its autumn tint of gold—
From the lightning in the sky
As it pass'd me flying by—
From the thunder, and the storm—
And the cloud that took the form
(When the rest of Heaven was blue)
Of a demon in my view—

To Helen

Helen, thy beauty is to me
  Like those Nicean barks of yore,
That gently, o'er a perfumed sea,
  The weary, way-worn wanderer bore
  To his own native shore.

On desperate seas long wont to roam,
  Thy hyacinth hair, thy classic face,
Thy Naiad airs have brought me home
  To the glory that was Greece,
And the grandeur that was Rome.

Lo! in yon brilliant window-niche
  How statue-like I see thee stand,
  The agate lamp within thy hand!
Ah, Psyche, from the regions which
  Are Holy-Land!

Israfel

*And the angel Israfel, whose heart-strings are a
lute, and who has the sweetest voice of all God's
creatures. —Koran*

In Heaven a spirit doth dwell
  "Whose heart-strings are a lute;"
None sing so wildly well
As the angel Israfel,
And the giddy stars (so legends tell)
Ceasing their hymns, attend the spell
  Of his voice, all mute.

Tottering above
   In her highest noon,
   The enamoured moon
Blushes with love,
   While, to listen, the red levin
   (With the rapid Pleiads, even,
   Which were seven,)
   Pauses in Heaven.

And they say (the starry choir
   And the other listening things)
That Israfeli's fire
Is owing to that lyre
   By which he sits and sings—
The trembling living wire
Of those unusual strings.

But the skies that angel trod,
   Where deep thoughts are a duty—
Where Love's a grown-up God—
   Where the Houri glances are
Imbued with all the beauty
   Which we worship in a star.

Therefore, thou art not wrong,
   Israfeli, who despisest
An unimpassioned song;
To thee the laurels belong,
   Best bard, because the wisest!
Merrily live, and long!

The ecstasies above
   With thy burning measures suit—
Thy grief, thy joy, thy hate, thy love,

With the fervour of thy lute—
Well may the stars be mute!

Yes, Heaven is thine; but this
 Is a world of sweets and sours;
 Our flowers are merely—flowers,
And the shadow of thy perfect bliss
 Is the sunshine of ours.

If I could dwell
Where Israfel
 Hath dwelt, and he where I,
He might not sing so wildly well
 A mortal melody,
While a bolder note than this might swell
 From my lyre within the sky.

The Sleeper

At midnight, in the month of June,
I stand beneath the mystic moon.
An opiate vapour, dewy, dim,
Exhales from out her golden rim,
And, softly dripping, drop by drop,
Upon the quiet mountain top,
Steals drowsily and musically
Into the universal valley.
The rosemary nods upon the grave;
The lily lolls upon the wave;
Wrapping the fog about its breast,
The ruin moulders into rest;
Looking like Lethe, see! the lake
A conscious slumber seems to take,

And would not, for the world, awake.
All Beauty sleeps!—and lo! where lies
Irene, with her Destinies!

Oh, lady bright! can it be right—
This window open to the night?
The wanton airs, from the tree-top,
Laughingly through the lattice drop—
The bodiless airs, a wizard rout,
Flit through thy chamber in and out,
And wave the curtain canopy
So fitfully—so fearfully—
Above the closed and fringed lid
'Neath which thy slumb'ring soul lies hid,
That, o'er the floor and down the wall,
Like ghosts the shadows rise and fall!
Oh, lady dear, hast thou no fear?
Why and what art thou dreaming here?
Sure thou art come o'er far-off seas,
A wonder to these garden trees!
Strange is thy pallor! strange thy dress!
Strange, above all, thy length of tress,
And this all solemn silentness!

The lady sleeps! Oh, may her sleep,
Which is enduring, so be deep!
Heaven have her in its sacred keep!
This chamber changed for one more holy,
This bed for one more melancholy,
I pray to God that she may lie
Forever with unopened eye,
While the pale sheeted ghosts go by!

My love, she sleeps! Oh, may her sleep,
As it is lasting, so be deep!
Soft may the worms about her creep!
Far in the forest, dim and old,
For her may some tall vault unfold—
Some vault that oft hath flung its black
And winged panels fluttering back,
Triumphant, o'er the crested palls,
Of her grand family funerals—
Some sepulchre, remote, alone,
Against whose portal she hath thrown,
In childhood, many an idle stone—
Some tomb from out whose sounding door
She ne'er shall force an echo more,
Thrilling to think, poor child of sin!
It was the dead who groaned within.

The Valley of Unrest

Once it smiled a silent dell
Where the people did not dwell;
They had gone unto the wars,
Trusting to the mild-eyed stars,
Nightly, from their azure towers,
To keep watch above the flowers,
In the midst of which all day
The red sun-light lazily lay.
Now each visiter shall confess
The sad valley's restlessness.
Nothing there is motionless.
Nothing save the airs that brood
Over the magic solitude.
Ah, by no wind are stirred those trees

That palpitate like the chill seas
Around the misty Hebrides!
Ah, by no wind those clouds are driven
That rustle through the unquiet Heaven
Uneasily, from morn till even,
Over the violets there that lie
In myriad types of the human eye—
Over the lilies there that wave
And weep above a nameless grave!
They wave:—from out their fragrant tops
Eternal dews come down in drops.
They weep:—from off their delicate stems
Perennial tears descend in gems.

The City in the Sea

Lo! Death has reared himself a throne
In a strange city lying alone
Far down within the dim West,
Where the good and the bad and the worst and the best
Have gone to their eternal rest.
There shrines and palaces and towers
(Time-eaten towers that tremble not!)
Resemble nothing that is ours.
Around, by lifting winds forgot,
Resignedly beneath the sky
The melancholy waters lie.

No rays from the holy heaven come down
On the long night-time of that town;
But light from out the lurid sea
Streams up the turrets silently—
Gleams up the pinnacles far and free

Up domes—up spires—up kingly halls—
Up fanes—up Babylon-like walls—
Up shadowy long-forgotten bowers
Of sculptured ivy and stone flowers—
Up many and many a marvellous shrine
Whose wreathed friezes intertwine
The viol, the violet, and the vine.
Resignedly beneath the sky
The melancholy waters lie.
So blend the turrets and shadows there
That all seem pendulous in air,
While from a proud tower in the town
Death looks gigantically down.

There open fanes and gaping graves
Yawn level with the luminous waves;
But not the riches there that lie
In each idol's diamond eye—
Not the gaily-jewelled dead
Tempt the waters from their bed;
For no ripples curl, alas!
Along that wilderness of glass—
No swellings tell that winds may be
Upon some far-off happier sea—
No heavings hint that winds have been
On seas less hideously serene.

But lo, a stir is in the air!
The wave—there is a movement there!
As if the towers had thrust aside,
In slightly sinking, the dull tide—
As if their tops had feebly given
A void within the filmy Heaven.
The waves have now a redder glow—

The hours are breathing faint and low—
And when, amid no earthly moans,
Down, down that town shall settle hence,
Hell, rising from a thousand thrones,
Shall do it reverence.

To One in Paradise

Thou wast that all to me, love,
    For which my soul did pine—
A green isle in the sea, love,
    A fountain and a shrine,
All wreathed with fairy fruits and flowers,
    And all the flowers were mine.

Ah, dream too bright to last!
    Ah, starry Hope! that didst arise
But to be overcast!
    A voice from out the Future cries
"On! on!"—but o'er the Past
    (Dim gulf!) my spirit hovering lies
Mute, motionless, aghast!

For, alas! alas! with me
    The light of Life is o'er!
No more—no more—no more—
(Such language holds the solemn sea
    To the sands upon the shore)
Shall bloom the thunder-blasted tree,
    Or the stricken eagle soar!

And all my days are trances,
    And all my nightly dreams

Are where thy grey eye glances,
    And where thy footstep gleams—
In what ethereal dances,
By what eternal streams.

The Coliseum

Type of the antique Rome! Rich reliquary
Of lofty contemplation left to Time
By buried centuries of pomp and power!
At length—at length—after so many days
Of weary pilgrimage and burning thirst,
(Thirst for the springs of lore that in thee lie,)
I kneel, an altered and an humble man,
Amid thy shadows, and so drink within
My very soul thy grandeur, gloom and glory!

Vastness! and Age! and Memories of Eld!
Silence! and Desolation! and dim Night!
I feel ye now—I feel ye in your strength—
O spells more sure than e'er Judaean king
Taught in the gardens of Gethsemane!
O charms more potent than the rapt Chaldee
Ever drew down from out the quiet stars!

Here, where a hero fell, a column falls!
Here, where the mimic eagle glared in gold,
A midnight vigil holds the swarthy bat!
Here, where the dames of Rome their gilded hair
Waved to the wind, now wave the reed and thistle!
Here, where on golden throne the monarch lolled,
Glides, spectre-like, unto his marble home,

Lit by the wan light of the horned moon,
The swift and silent lizard of the stones!

But stay! these walls—these ivy-clad arcades—
These mouldering plinths—these sad and blackened shafts—
These vague entablatures—this crumbling frieze—
These shattered cornices—this wreck—this ruin—
These stones—alas! these grey stones—are they all—
All of the famed, and the colossal left
By the corrosive Hours to Fate and me?

"Not all"—the Echoes answer me—"not all!
"Prophetic sounds and loud, arise forever
"From us, and from all Ruin, unto the wise,
"As melody from Memnon to the Sun.
"We rule the hearts of mightiest men—we rule
"With a despotic sway all giant minds.
"We are not impotent—we pallid stones.
"Not all our power is gone—not all our fame—
"Not all the magic of our high renown—
"Not all the wonder that encircles us—
"Not all the mysteries that in us lie—
"Not all the memories that hang upon
"And cling around about us as a garment,
"Clothing us in a robe of more than glory."

Bridal Ballad

The ring is on my hand,
    And the wreath is on my brow;
Satins and jewels grand
Are all at my command,
    And I am happy now.

And my lord he loves me well;
   But when he breathed his vow,
I felt my bosom swell—
For the words rang as a knell,
And the voice seemed *his* who fell
In the battle down the dell,
   And who is happy now.

But he spoke to re-assure me,
   And he kissed my pallid brow,
While a reverie came o'er me,
And to the church-yard bore me,
And I sighed to him before me,
(Thinking him dead D'Elormie,)
   "Oh, I am happy now!"

And thus the words were spoken;
   And this the plighted vow;
And, though my faith be broken,
And, though my heart be broken,
Here is a ring, as token
   That I am happy now!—
Behold the golden token
   That *proves* me happy now!

Would God I could awaken!
   For I dream I know not how,
And my soul is sorely shaken
Lest an evil step be taken,—
Lest the dead who is forsaken
   May not be happy now.

The Haunted Palace

In the greenest of our valleys
    By good angels tenanted,
Once a fair and stately palace—
    Radiant palace—reared its head.
In the monarch Thought's dominion—
    It stood there!
Never seraph spread a pinion
    Over fabric half so fair!

Banners yellow, glorious, golden,
    On its roof did float and flow—
(This—all this—was in the olden
    Time long ago)
And every gentle air that dallied,
    In that sweet day,
Along the ramparts plumed and pallid,
    A wingéd odor went away.

Wanderers in that happy valley,
    Through two luminous windows, saw
Spirits moving musically,
    To a lute's well-tunéd law,
Round about a throne where, sitting,
    Porphyrogene,
In state his glory well befitting
    The ruler of the realm was seen.

And all with pearl and ruby glowing
    Was the fair palace door,
Through which came flowing, flowing, flowing,
    And sparkling evermore,
A troop of Echoes whose sweet duty

Was but to sing,
In voices of surpassing beauty,
    The wit and wisdom of their king.

But evil things, in robes of sorrow,
    Assailed the monarch's high estate.
(Ah, let us mourn!—for never morrow
    Shall dawn upon him, desolate!)
And round about his home the glory
    That blushed and bloomed,
Is but a dim-remembered story
    Of the old-time entombed.

And travellers, now, within that valley,
    Through the encrimsoned windows see
Vast forms that move fantastically
    To a discordant melody,
While, like a ghastly rapid river,
    Through the pale door
A hideous throng rush out forever
    And laugh—but smile no more.

Sonnet—Silence

There are some qualities—some incorporate things,
    That have a double life, which thus is made
A type of that twin entity which springs
    From matter and light, evinced in solid and shade.
There is a two-fold *Silence*—sea and shore—
    Body and Soul. One dwells in lonely places,
    Newly with grass o'ergrown; some solemn graces,
Some human memories and tearful lore,
Render him terrorless: his name's "No more."

He is the corporate Silence: dread him not!
   No power hath he of evil in himself;
But should some urgent fate (untimely lot!)
   Bring thee to meet his shadow (nameless elf,
That haunteth the lone regions where hath trod
No foot of man,) commend thyself to God!

The Conqueror Worm

Lo! 'tis a gala night
   Within the lonesome latter years!
And angel throng, bewinged, bedight
   In veils, and drowned in tears,
Sit in a theatre, to see
   A play of hopes and fears,
While the orchestra breathes fitfully
   The music of the spheres.

Mimes, in the form of God on high,
   Mutter and mumble low,
And hither and thither fly—
   Mere puppets they, who come and go
At bidding of vast formless things
   That shift the scenery to and fro,
Flapping from out their Condor wings
   Invisible Wo!

That motley drama—oh, be sure
   It shall not be forgot!
With its Phantom chased for evermore,
   By a crowd that seize it not,
Through a circle that ever returneth in
   To the self-same spot,

And much of Madness, and more of Sin,
    And Horror the soul of the plot.

But see, amid the mimic rout
    A crawling shape intrude!
A blood-red thing that writhes from out
    The scenic solitude!
It writhes!—it writhes!—with mortal pangs
    The mimes become its food,
And seraphs sob at vermin fangs
In human gore imbued.

Out—out are the lights—out all!
    And, over each quivering form,
The curtain, a funeral pall,
    Comes down with the rush of a storm,
While the angels, all pallid and wan,
    Uprising, unveiling, affirm
That the play is the tragedy, "Man,"
    And its hero the Conqueror Worm.

Lenore

Ah, broken is the golden bowl!—the spirit flown forever!
Let the bell toll!—a saintly soul floats on the Stygian river:—
And, Guy De Vere, hast *thou* no tear?—weep now or never more!
See! on yon drear and rigid bier low lies thy love, Lenore!
Come, let the burial rite be read—the funeral song be sung!—
An anthem for the queenliest dead that ever died so young—
A dirge for her the doubly dead in that she died so young.

"Wretches! ye loved her for her wealth and ye hated her for her
    pride;

And, when she fell in feeble health, ye blessed her—that she
    died:—
How *shall* the ritual then be read—the requiem how be sung
By you—by yours, the evil eye—by yours the slanderous tongue
That did to death the innocence that died and died so young?"

Peccavimus:—yet rave not thus! but let a Sabbath song
Go up to God so solemnly the dead may feel no wrong!
The sweet Lenore hath gone before, with Hope that flew beside,
Leaving thee wild for the dear child that should have been thy
    bride—
For her, the fair and debonair, that now so lowly lies,
The life upon her yellow hair, but not within her eyes—
The life still there upon her hair, the death upon her eyes.

"Avaunt!—avaunt! to friends from fiends the indignant ghost is
    riven—
From Hell unto a high estate within the utmost Heaven—
From moan and groan to a golden throne beside the King of
    Heaven:—
Let *no* bell toll, then, lest her soul, amid its hallowed mirth
Should catch the note as it doth float up from the damned Earth!
And I—tonight my heart is light:—no dirge will I upraise,
But waft the angel on her flight with a Paean of old days!"

Dream-Land

By a route obscure and lonely,
Haunted by ill angels only,
Where an Eidolon, named Night,
On a black throne reigns upright,
I have reached these lands but newly
From an ultimate dim Thule—

From a wild weird clime that lieth, sublime,
 Out of Space—out of Time.

 Bottomless vales and boundless floods,
 And chasms, and caves, and Titan woods,
 With forms that no man can discover
 For the dews that drip all over;
 Mountains toppling evermore
 Into seas without a shore;
 Seas that restlessly aspire,
 Surging, unto skies of fire;
 Lakes that endlessly outspread
 Their lone waters—lone and dead,—
 Their still waters—still and chilly
 With the snows of the lolling lily.

 By the lakes that thus outspread
 Their lone waters, lone and dead,—
 Their sad waters, sad and chilly
 With the snows of the lolling lily,—
 By the mountains—near the river
 Murmuring lowly, murmuring ever,—
 By the grey woods,—by the swamp
 Where the toad and the newt encamp,—
 By the dismal tarns and pools
  Where dwell the Ghouls,—
 By each spot the most unholy—
 In each nook most melancholy,—
 There the traveller meets aghast
 Sheeted Memories of the Past—
 Shrouded forms that start and sigh
 As they pass the wanderer by—
 White-robed forms of friends long given,
 In agony, to the Earth—and Heaven.

For the heart whose woes are legion
'Tis a peaceful, soothing region—
For the spirit that walks in shadow
O! it is an Eldorado!
But the traveller, travelling through it,
May not—dare not openly view it;
Never its mysteries are exposed
To the weak human eye unclosed;
So wills its King, who hath forbid
The uplifting of the fringed lid;
And thus the sad Soul that here passes
Beholds it but through darkened glasses.

By a route obscure and lonely,
Haunted by ill angels only,
Where an Eidolon, named NIGHT,
On a black throne reigns upright,
I have wandered home but newly
From this ultimate dim Thule.

Eulalie—A Song

I dwelt alone
In a world of moan,
And my soul was a stagnant tide
Till the fair and gentle Eulalie became my blushing bride—
Till the yellow-haired young Eulalie became my smiling bride.

Ah, less, less bright
The stars of the night
Than the eyes of the radiant girl,
And never a flake

That the vapor can make
With the moon-tints of purple and pearl
Can vie with the modest Eulalie's most unregarded curl—
Can compare with the bright-eyed Eulalie's most humble and
careless curl.

Now Doubt—now Pain
Come never again,
For her soul gives me sigh for sigh
And all day long
Shines bright and strong
Astarte within the sky,
While ever to her dear Eulalie upturns her matron eye—
While ever to her young Eulalie upturns her violet eye.

The Raven

Once upon a midnight dreary, while I pondered, weak and weary,
Over many a quaint and curious volume of forgotten lore—
While I nodded, nearly napping, suddenly there came a tapping,
As of some one gently rapping, rapping at my chamber door—
" 'Tis some visiter," I muttered, "tapping at my chamber door—
Only this and nothing more."

Ah, distinctly I remember it was in the bleak December;
And each separate dying ember wrought its ghost upon the floor.
Eagerly I wished the morrow;—vainly I had sought to borrow
From my books surcease of sorrow—sorrow for the lost Lenore—
For the rare and radiant maiden whom the angels name Lenore—
Nameless *here* for evermore.

And the silken, sad, uncertain rustling of each purple curtain
Thrilled me—filled me with fantastic terrors never felt before;
So that now, to still the beating of my heart, I stood repeating
" 'Tis some visiter entreating entrance at my chamber door—
Some late visiter entreating entrance at my chamber door;—
   This it is and nothing more."

Presently my soul grew stronger; hesitating then no longer,
"Sir," said I, "or Madam, truly your forgiveness I implore;
But the fact is I was napping, and so gently you came rapping,
And so faintly you came tapping, tapping at my chamber door,
That I scarce was sure I heard you"—here I opened wide the
  door;——
   Darkness there and nothing more.

Deep into that darkness peering, long I stood there wondering,
  fearing,
Doubting, dreaming dreams no mortal ever dared to dream before;
But the silence was unbroken, and the stillness gave no token,
And the only word there spoken was the whispered word,
  "Lenore?"
This I whispered, and an echo murmured back the word, "Lenore!"
   Merely this and nothing more.

Back into the chamber turning, all my soul within me burning,
Soon again I heard a tapping somewhat louder than before.
"Surely," said I, "surely that is something at my window lattice;
Let me see, then, what thereat is, and this mystery explore—
Let my heart be still a moment and this mystery explore;—
   'Tis the wind and nothing more!"

Open here I flung the shutter, when, with many a flirt and flutter,
In there stepped a stately Raven of the saintly days of yore;
Not the least obeisance made he; not a minute stopped or stayed he;

But, with mien of lord or lady, perched above my chamber door—
Perched upon a bust of Pallas just above my chamber door—
     Perched, and sat, and nothing more.

Then this ebony bird beguiling my sad fancy into smiling,
By the grave and stern decorum of the countenance it wore,
"Though thy crest be shorn and shaven, thou," I said, "art sure no
    craven,
Ghastly grim and ancient Raven wandering from the Nightly
    shore—
Tell me what thy lordly name is on the Night's Plutonian shore!"
     Quoth the Raven "Nevermore."

Much I marvelled this ungainly fowl to hear discourse so plainly,
Though its answer little meaning—little relevancy bore;
For we cannot help agreeing that no living human being
Ever yet was blessed with seeing bird above his chamber door—
Bird or beast upon the sculptured bust above his chamber door,
     With such a name as "Nevermore."

But the Raven, sitting lonely on the placid bust, spoke only
That one word, as if his soul in that one word he did outpour.
Nothing farther then he uttered—not a feather then he fluttered—
Till I scarcely more than muttered "Other friends have flown
    before—
On the morrow *he* will leave me, as my Hopes have flown before."
     Then the bird said "Nevermore."

Startled at the stillness broken by reply so aptly spoken,
"Doubtless," said I, "what it utters is its only stock and store
Caught from some unhappy master whom unmerciful Disaster
Followed fast and followed faster till his songs one burden bore—
Till the dirges of his Hope that melancholy burden bore
     Of 'Never—nevermore.' "

But the Raven still beguiling my sad fancy into smiling,
Straight I wheeled a cushioned seat in front of bird, and bust and
 door;
Then, upon the velvet sinking, I betook myself to linking
Fancy unto fancy, thinking what this ominous bird of yore—
What this grim, ungainly, ghastly, gaunt, and ominous bird of yore
 Meant in croaking "Nevermore."

This I sat engaged in guessing, but no syllable expressing
To the fowl whose fiery eyes now burned into my bosom's core;
This and more I sat divining, with my head at ease reclining
On the cushion's velvet lining that the lamp-light gloated o'er,
But whose velvet-violet lining with the lamp-light gloating o'er,
 She shall press, ah, nevermore!

Then, methought, the air grew denser, perfumed from an unseen
 censer
Swung by seraphim whose foot-falls tinkled on the tufted floor.
"Wretch," I cried, "thy God hath lent thee—by these angels he
 hath sent thee
Respite—respite and nepenthe from thy memories of Lenore;
Quaff, oh quaff this kind nepenthe and forget this lost Lenore!"
 Quoth the Raven "Nevermore."

"Prophet!" said I, "thing of evil!—prophet still, if bird or devil!—
Whether Tempter sent, or whether tempest tossed thee here ashore,
Desolate yet all undaunted, on this desert land enchanted—
On this home by Horror haunted—tell me truly, I implore—
Is there—*is* there balm in Gilead?—tell me—tell me, I implore!"
 Quoth the Raven "Nevermore."

"Prophet!" said I, "thing of evil!—prophet still, if bird or devil!
By that Heaven that bends above us—by that God we both
 adore—

Tell this soul with sorrow laden if, within the distant Aidenn,
It shall clasp a sainted maiden whom the angels name Lenore—
Clasp a rare and radiant maiden whom the angels name Lenore."
        Quoth the Raven "Nevermore."

"Be that word our sign of parting, bird or fiend!" I shrieked,
    upstarting—
"Get thee back into the tempest and the Night's Plutonian shore!
Leave no black plume as a token of that lie thy soul hath spoken!
Leave my loneliness unbroken!—quit the bust above my door!
Take thy beak from out my heart, and take thy form from off my
    door!"
        Quoth the Raven "Nevermore."

And the Raven, never flitting, still is sitting, *still* is sitting
On the pallid bust of Pallas just above my chamber door;
And his eyes have all the seeming of a demon's that is dreaming,
And the lamp-light o'er him streaming throws his shadow on the
    floor;
And my soul from out that shadow that lies floating on the floor
        Shall be lifted—nevermore!

A Valentine to————

For her this rhyme is penned, whose luminous eyes,
    Brightly expressive as the twins of Laeda,
Shall find her own sweet name, that, nestling lies
    Upon the page, enwrapped from every reader.
Search narrowly the lines!—they hold a treasure
    Divine—a talisman—an amulet
That must be worn *at heart*. Search well the measure—
    The words—the syllables! Do not forget
The trivialest point, or you may lose your labor!

And yet there is in this no Gordian knot
Which one might not undo without a sabre,
  If one could merely comprehend the plot.
Enwritten upon the leaf where now are peering
  Eyes scintillating soul, there lie *perdus*
Three eloquent words oft uttered in the hearing
  Of poets, by poets—as the name is a poet's, too.
Its letters, although naturally lying
  Like the knight Pinto—Mendez Ferdinando—
Still form a synonym for Truth.—Cease trying!
  You will not read the riddle, though you do the best you
    can do.

Ulalume—A Ballad

The skies they were ashen and sober;
  The leaves they were crispéd and sere—
  The leaves they were withering and sere:
It was night, in the lonesome October
  Of my most immemorial year:
It was hard by the dim lake of Auber,
  In the misty mid region of Weir:—
It was down by the dank tarn of Auber,
  In the ghoul-haunted woodland of Weir.

Here once, through an alley Titanic,
  Of cypress, I roamed with my Soul—
  Of cypress, with Psyche, my Soul.
These were days when my heart was volcanic
  As the scoriac rivers that roll—
  As the lavas that restlessly roll
Their sulphurous currents down Yaanek,
  In the ultimate climes of the Pole—

That groan as they roll down Mount Yaanek,
    In the realms of the Boreal Pole.

Our talk had been serious and sober,
    But our thoughts they were palsied and sere—
    Our memories were treacherous and sere;
For we knew not the month was October,
    And we marked not the night of the year—
    (Ah, night of all nights in the year!)
We noted not the dim lake of Auber,
    (Though once we had journeyed down here)
We remembered not the dank tarn of Auber,
    Nor the ghoul-haunted woodland of Weir.

And now, as the night was senescent,
    And star-dials pointed to morn—
    As the star-dials hinted of morn—
At the end of our path a liquescent
    And nebulous lustre was born,
Out of which a miraculous crescent
    Arose with a duplicate horn—
Astarte's bediamonded crescent,
    Distinct with its duplicate horn.

And I said—"She is warmer than Dian;
    She rolls through an ether of sighs—
    She revels in a region of sighs.
She has seen that the tears are not dry on
    These cheeks where the worm never dies,
And has come past the stars of the Lion,
    To point us the path to the skies—
    To the Lethean peace of the skies—
Come up, in despite of the Lion,
    To shine on us with her bright eyes—

Come up, through the lair of the Lion,
   With love in her luminous eyes."

But Psyche, uplifting her finger,
   Said—"Sadly this star I mistrust—
   Her pallor I strangely mistrust—
Ah, hasten!—ah, let us not linger!
   Ah, fly!—let us fly!—for we must."
In terror she spoke; letting sink her
   Wings till they trailed in the dust—
In agony sobbed; letting sink her
   Plumes till they trailed in the dust—
   Till they sorrowfully trailed in the dust.

I replied—"This is nothing but dreaming.
   Let us on, by this tremulous light!
   Let us bathe in this crystalline light!
Its Sibyllic splendor is beaming
   With Hope and in Beauty to-night—
   See!—it flickers up the sky through the night!
Ah, we safely may trust to its gleaming
   And be sure it will lead us aright—
We surely may trust to a gleaming
   That cannot but guide us aright
Since it flickers up to Heaven through the night."

Thus I pacified Psyche and kissed her,
   And tempted her out of her gloom—
   And conquered her scruples and gloom;
And we passed to the end of the vista—
   But were stopped by the door of a tomb—
   By the door of a legended tomb:—
And I said—"What is written, sweet sister,
   On the door of this legended tomb?"

She replied—"Ulalume—Ulalume!—
'Tis the vault of thy lost Ulalume!"

Then my heart it grew ashen and sober
    As the leaves that were crispéd and sere—
    As the leaves that were withering and sere—
And I cried—"It was surely October,
    On *this* very night of last year,
    That I journeyed—I journeyed down here!—
    That I brought a dread burden down here—
    On this night, of all nights in the year,
    Ah, what demon hath tempted me here?
Well I know, now, this dim lake of Auber—
    This misty mid region of Weir:—
Well I know, now, this dark tarn of Auber—
    This ghoul-haunted woodland of Weir."

Said we, then—the two, then—"Ah, can it
    Have been that the woodlandish ghouls—
    The pitiful, the merciful ghouls,
To bar up our way and to ban it
    From the secret that lies in these wolds—
    From the thing that lies hidden in these wolds—
Have drawn up the spectre of a planet
    From the limbo of lunary souls—
This sinfully scintillant planet
    From the Hell of the planetary souls?"

The Bells

1.

Hear the sledges with the bells—
Silver bells!
What a world of merriment their melody foretells!
How they tinkle, tinkle, tinkle.
In the icy air of night!
While the stars that oversprinkle
All the Heavens, seem to twinkle
With a crystalline delight;
Keeping time, time, time,
In a sort of Runic rhyme,
To the tintinabulation that so musically wells
From the bells, bells, bells, bells,
Bells, bells, bells—
From the jingling and the tinkling of the bells.

2.

Hear the mellow wedding bells—
Golden bells!
What a world of happiness their harmony foretells!
Through the balmy air of night
How they ring out their delight!—
From the molten-golden notes
And all in tune,
What a liquid ditty floats
To the turtle-dove that listens while she gloats
On the moon!
Oh, from out the sounding cells
What a gush of euphony voluminously wells!
How it swells!
How it dwells
On the Future!—how it tells

Of the rapture that impels
To the swinging and the ringing
  Of the bells, bells, bells!—
Of the bells, bells, bells, bells,
    Bells, bells, bells—
To the rhyming and the chiming of the bells!

3.

Hear the loud alarum bells—
    Brazen bells!
What tale of terror, now, their turbulency tells!
  In the startled ear of Night
  How they scream out their affright!
    Too much horrified to speak,
    They can only shriek, shriek,
      Out of tune,
In a clamorous appealing to the mercy of the fire—
In a mad expostulation with the deaf and frantic fire,
      Leaping higher, higher, higher,
      With a desperate desire
    And a resolute endeavor
    Now—now to sit, or never,
By the side of the pale-faced moon.
      Oh, the bells, bells, bells!
      What a tale their terror tells
        Of despair!
  How they clang and clash and roar!
  What a horror they outpour
  In the bosom of the palpitating air!
      Yet the ear, it fully knows,
        By the twanging
        And the clanging,
      How the danger ebbs and flows:—
  Yes, the ear distinctly tells,

In the jangling
And the wrangling,
How the danger sinks and swells,
By the sinking or the swelling in the anger of the bells—
Of the bells—
Of the bells, bells, bells, bells,
Bells, bells, bells—
In the clamor and the clangor of the bells.

4.

Hear the tolling of the bells—
Iron bells!
What a world of solemn thought their monody compels!
In the silence of the night
How we shiver with affright
At the melancholy meaning of the tone!
For every sound that floats
From the rust within their throats
Is a groan.
And the people—ah, the people
They that dwell up in the steeple
All alone,
And who, tolling, tolling, tolling,
In that muffled monotone,
Feel a glory in so rolling
On the human heart a stone—
They are neither man nor woman—
They are neither brute nor human,
They are Ghouls:—
And their king it is who tolls:—
And he rolls, rolls, rolls, rolls
A Pæan from the bells!
And his merry bosom swells
With the Pæan of the bells!

And he dances and he yells;
Keeping time, time, time,
In a sort of Runic rhyme,
To the Pæan of the bells—
Of the bells:—
Keeping time, time, time,
In a sort of Runic rhyme,
To the throbbing of the bells—
Of the bells, bells, bells—
To the sobbing of the bells:—
Keeping time, time, time,
As he knells, knells, knells,
In a happy Runic rhyme,
To the rolling of the bells—
Of the bells, bells, bells:—
To the tolling of the bells—
Of the bells, bells, bells, bells,
Bells, bells, bells—
To the moaning and the groaning of the bells.

To Helen

I saw thee once—once only—years ago:
I must not say *how* many—but *not* many.
It was a July midnight; and from out
A full-orbed moon, that, like thine own soul, soaring,
Sought a precipitate pathway up through heaven,
There fell a silvery-silken veil of light,
With quietude, and sultriness, and slumber,
Upon the upturn'd faces of a thousand
Roses that grew in an enchanted garden,
Where no wind dared to stir, unless on tiptoe—
Fell on the upturn'd faces of these roses

That gave out, in return for the love-light,
Their odorous souls in an ecstatic death—
Fell on the upturn'd faces of these roses
That smiled and died in this parterre, enchanted
By thee, and by the poetry of thy presence.

Clad all in white, upon a violet bank
I saw thee half reclining; while the moon
Fell on the upturn'd faces of the roses,
And on thine own, upturn'd—alas, in sorrow!

Was it not Fate, that, on this July midnight—
Was it not Fate, (whose name is also Sorrow,)
That bade me pause before that garden-gate,
To breathe the incense of those slumbering roses?
No footstep stirred: the hated world all slept,
Save only thee and me. (Oh, Heaven!—oh, God!
How my heart beats in coupling those two words!)
Save only thee and me. I paused—I looked—
And in an instant all things disappeared.
(Ah, bear in mind this garden was enchanted!)
The pearly lustre of the moon went out:
The mossy banks and the meandering paths,
The happy flowers and the repining trees,
Were seen no more: the very roses' odors
Died in the arms of the adoring airs.
All—all expired save thee—save less than thou:
Save only the divine light in thine eyes—
Save but the soul in thine uplifted eyes.
I saw but them—they were the world to me.
I saw but them—saw only them for hours—
Saw only them until the moon went down.
What wild heart-histories seemed to lie enwritten
Upon those crystalline, celestial spheres!

How dark a wo! yet how sublime a hope!
How silently serene a sea of pride!
How daring an ambition! yet how deep—
How fathomless a capacity for love!

But now, at length, dear Dian sank from sight,
Into a western couch of thunder-cloud;
And thou, a ghost, amid the entombing trees
Didst glide away. *Only thine eyes remained.*
They *would not* go—they never yet have gone.
Lighting my lonely pathway home that night,
They have not left me (as my hopes have) since.
They follow me—they lead me through the years.
They are my ministers—yet I their slave.
Their office is to illumine and enkindle—
My duty, *to be saved* by their bright light,
And purified in their electric fire,
And sanctified in their elysian fire.
They fill my soul with Beauty (which is Hope,)
And are far up in Heaven—the stars I kneel to
In the sad, silent watches of the night;
While even in the meridian glare of day
I see them still—two sweetly scintillant
Venuses, unextinguished by the sun!

A Dream Within a Dream

Take this kiss upon the brow!
And, in parting from you now,
Thus much let me avow—
You are not wrong, who deem
That my days have been a dream;
Yet if hope has flown away

In a night, or in a day,
In a vision, or in none,
Is it therefore the less *gone?*
All that we see or seem
Is but a dream within a dream.

I stand amid the roar
Of a surf-tormented shore,
And I hold within my hand
Grains of the golden sand—
How few! yet how they creep
Through my fingers to the deep,
While I weep—while I weep!
O God! can I not grasp
Them with a tighter clasp?
O God! can I not save
One from the pitiless wave?
Is *all* that we see or seem
But a dream within a dream?

For Annie

Thank Heaven! the crisis—
   The danger is past,
And the lingering illness
   Is over at last—
And the fever called "Living"
   Is conquered at last.

Sadly, I know
   I am shorn of my strength,
And no muscle I move
   As I lie at full length—

But no matter!—I feel
  I am better at length.

And I rest so composedly,
  Now, in my bed,
That any beholder
  Might fancy me dead—
Might start at beholding me,
  Thinking me dead.

The moaning and groaning,
  The sighing and sobbing,
Are quieted now,
  With that horrible throbbing
At heart:—ah, that horrible,
  Horrible throbbing!

The sickness—the nausea—
  The pitiless pain—
Have ceased, with the fever
  That maddened my brain—
With the fever called "Living"
  That burned in my brain.

And oh! of all tortures
  That torture the worst
Has abated—the terrible
  Torture of thirst
For the napthaline river
  Of Passion accurst:—
I have drank of a water
  That quenches all thirst:—

Of a water that flows,
  With a lullaby sound,
From a spring but a very few
  Feet under ground—
From a cavern not very far
  Down under ground.

And ah! let it never
  Be foolishly said
That my room it is gloomy
  And narrow my bed;
For man never slept
  In a different bed—
And, to *sleep,* you must slumber
  In just such a bed.

My tantalized spirit
  Here blandly reposes,
Forgetting, or never
  Regretting its roses—
Its old agitations
  Of myrtles and roses:

For now, while so quietly
  Lying, it fancies
A holier odor
  About it, of pansies—
A rosemary odor,
  Commingled with pansies—
With rue and the beautiful
  Puritan pansies.

And so it lies happily,
  Bathing in many

A dream of the truth
   And the beauty of Annie—
Drowned in a bath
   Of the tresses of Annie.

She tenderly kissed me,
   She fondly caressed,
And then I fell gently
   To sleep on her breast—
Deeply to sleep
   From the heaven of her breast.

When the light was extinguished,
   She covered me warm,
And she prayed to the angels
   To keep me from harm—
To the queen of the angels
   To shield me from harm.

And I lie so composedly,
   Now, in my bed,
(Knowing her love)
   That you fancy me dead—
And I rest so contentedly,
   Now in my bed,
(With her love at my breast)
   That you fancy me dead—
That you shudder to look at me,
   Thinking me dead:—

But my heart it is brighter
   Than all of the many
Stars in the sky,
   For it sparkles with Annie—

It glows with the light
   Of the love of my Annie—
With the thought of the light
   Of the eyes of my Annie.

Eldorado

   Gaily bedight,
   A gallant knight,
In sunshine and in shadow,
   Had journeyed long,
   Singing a song,
In search of Eldorado.

   But he grew old—
   This knight so bold—
And o'er his heart a shadow
   Fell, as he found
   No spot of ground
That looked like Eldorado.

   And, as his strength
   Failed him at length
He met a pilgrim shadow—
   "Shadow," said he,
   "Where can it be—
This land of Eldorado?"

   "Over the Mountains
   Of the Moon,
Down the Valley of the Shadow,
   Ride, boldly ride,"

The shade replied,—
"If you seek for Eldorado!"

To My Mother

Because the angels in the Heavens above,
    Devoutly singing unto one another,
Can find, amid their burning terms of love,
    None so devotional as that of "mother,"
Therefore by that sweet name I long have called you;
    You who are more than mother unto me,
Filling my heart of hearts, where God installed you,
    In setting my Virginia's spirit free.
My mother—my own mother, who died early,
    Was but the mother of myself; but you
Are mother to the dead I loved so dearly,
    Are thus more precious than the one I knew,
By that infinity with which my wife
Was dearer to my soul than its soul-life.

Annabel Lee

It was many and many a year ago,
    In a kingdom by the sea,
That a maiden there lived whom you may know
    By the name of Annabel Lee;—
And this maiden she lived with no other thought
    Than to love and be loved by me.

I was a child and *she* was a child,
    In this kingdom by the sea;
But we loved with a love that was more than love—

   I and my Annabel Lee—
With a love that the wingéd seraphs in Heaven
   Coveted her and me.

And this was the reason that, long ago,
   In this kingdom by the sea,
A wind blew out of a cloud, chilling
   My beautiful Annabel Lee;
So that her high-born kinsmen came
   And bore her away from me,
To shut her up in a sepulchre,
   In this kingdom by the sea.

The angels, not half so happy in Heaven,
   Went envying her and me—
Yes!—that was the reason (as all men know,
   In this kingdom by the sea)
That the wind came out of the cloud by night,
   Chilling and killing my Annabel Lee.

But our love it was stronger by far than the love
   Of those who were older than we—
   Of many far wiser than we—
And neither the angels in Heaven above,
   Nor the demons down under the sea,
Can ever dissever my soul from the soul
   Of the beautiful Annabel Lee:—

For the moon never beams, without bringing me dreams
   Of the beautiful Annabel Lee;
And the stars never rise, but I feel the bright eyes
   Of the beautiful Annabel Lee:—
And so, all the night-tide, I lie down by the side
Of my darling—my darling—my life and my bride,

In her sepulchre there by the sea—
In her tomb by the sounding sea.

LETTER TO B———.

West Point, ——— 1831.

Dear B———.

*   *   *

Believing only a portion of my former volume to be worthy a second edition—that small portion I thought it as well to include in the present book as to republish by itself. I have, therefore, herein combined Al Aaraaf and Tamerlane with other Poems hitherto unprinted. Nor have I hesitated to insert from the "Minor Poems," now omitted, whole lines, and even passages, to the end that being placed in a fairer light, and the trash shaken from them in which they were imbedded, they may have some chance of being seen by posterity.

*   *   *

It has been said, that a good critique on a poem may be written by one who is no poet himself. This, according to your ideas and mine of poetry, I feel to be false—the less poetical the critic, the less just the critique, and the converse. Of this account, and because there are but few B———s in the world, I would be as much ashamed of the world's good opinion, as proud of your own. Another than yourself might here observe "Shakespeare is in possession of the world's good opinion, and yet Shakespeare is the greatest of poets. It appears then that the world judge correctly, why should you be ashamed of their favorable judgment?" The difficulty lies in the interpretation of the word "judgment" or "opinion." The opinion is the world's, truly, but it may be called theirs as a man would call a book his, having bought it; he did not write the book, but it is his; they did not originate the opinion, but it is theirs. A fool, for example, thinks Shakespeare a great poet—yet the fool has never read Shakespeare. But the fool's neighbor, who is a step higher

on the Andes of the mind, whose head (that is to say his more exalted thought) is too far above the fool to be seen or understood, but whose feet (by which I mean his every day actions) are sufficiently near to be discerned, and by means of which that superiority is ascertained, which but for them would never have been discovered—this neighbor asserts that Shakespeare is a great poet—the fool believes him, and it is henceforward his opinion. This neighbor's own opinion has, in like manner, been adopted from one above him, and so, ascendingly, to a few gifted individuals, who kneel around the summit, beholding, face to face, the master spirit who stands upon the pinnacle.

*   *   *

You are aware of the great barrier in the path of an American writer. He is read, if at all, in preference to the combined and established wit of the world. I say established; for it is with literature as with law or empire—an established name is an estate in tenure, or a throne in possession. Besides, one might suppose that books, like their authors, improve by travel—their having crossed the sea is, with us, so great a distinction. Our antiquaries abandon time for distance; our very fops glance from the binding to the bottom of the title-page, where the mystic characters which spell London, Paris, or Genoa, are precisely so many letters of recommendation.

*   *   *

I mentioned just now a vulgar error as regards criticism. I think the notion that no poet can form a correct estimate of his own writings is another. I remarked before, that in proportion to the poetical talent, would be the justice of a critique upon poetry. Therefore, a bad poet would, I grant, make a false critique, and his self-love would infallibly bias his little judgment in his favor; but a poet, who is indeed a poet, could not, I think, fail of making a just critique. Whatever should be deducted on the score of self-love, might be replaced on account of his intimate acquaintance with the subject; in short, we have more instances of false criticism than of just, where one's own writings are the test,

simply because we have more bad poets than good. There are of course many objections to what I say: Milton is a great example of the contrary; but his opinion with respect to the Paradise Regained, is by no means fairly ascertained. By what trivial circumstances men are often led to assert what they do not really believe! Perhaps an inadvertent work has descended to posterity. But, in fact, the Paradise Regained is little, if at all, inferior to the Paradise Lost, and is only supposed so to be because men do not like epics, whatever they may say to the contrary, and reading those of Milton in their natural order, are too much wearied with the first to derive any pleasure from the second.

I dare say Milton preferred Comus to either—if so—justly.

* * *

As I am speaking of poetry, it will not be amiss to touch slightly upon the most singular heresy in its modern history—the heresy of what is called very foolishly, the Lake School. Some years ago I might have been induced, by an occasion like the present, to attempt a formal refutation of their doctrine; at present it would be a work of superogation. The wise must bow to the wisdom of such men as Coleridge and Southey, but being wise, have laughed at poetical theories so prosaically exemplified.

Aristotle, with singular assurance, has declared poetry the most philosophical of all writing—but it required a Wordsworth to pronounce it the most metaphysical. He seems to think that the end of poetry is, or should be, instruction—yet it is a truism that the end of our existence is happiness; if so, the end of every separate part of our existence—every thing connected with our existence should be happiness; and happiness is another name for pleasure;—therefore the end of instruction should be pleasure: yet we see the above mentioned opinion implies precisely the reverse.

To proceed: *ceteris paribus,* he who pleases, is of more importance to his fellow men than he who instructs, since utility is happiness, and pleasure is the end already obtained which instruction is merely the means of obtaining.

I see no reason, then, why our metaphysical poets should plume themselves so much on the utility of their works, unless indeed they refer to instruction with eternity in view; in which case, sincere respect for their piety would not allow me to express my contempt for their judgment; contempt which it would be difficult to conceal, since their writings are professedly to be understood by the few, and it is the many who stand in need of salvation. In such case I should no doubt be tempted to think of the devil in *Melmoth,* who labors indefatigably through three octavo volumes, to accomplish the destruction of one or two souls, while any common devil would have demolished one or two thousand.

*   *   *

Against the subtleties which would make poetry a study—not a passion—it becomes the metaphysician to reason—but the poet to protest. Yet Wordsworth and Coleridge are men in years; the one imbued in contemplation from his childhood, the other a giant in intellect and learning. The diffidence, then, with which I venture to dispute their authority would be overwhelming, did I not feel, from the bottom of my heart, that learning has little to do with the imagination—intellect with the passions—or age with poetry. . . .

"Trifles, like straws, upon the surface flow,
He who would search for pearls must dive below,"

are lines which have done much mischief. As regards the greater truths, men oftener err by seeking them at the bottom than at the top; the depth lies in the huge abysses where wisdom is sought—not in the palpable palaces where she is found. The ancients were not always right in hiding the goddess in a well: witness the light which Bacon has thrown upon philosophy; witness the principles of our divine faith—that moral mechanism by which the simplicity of a child may overbalance the wisdom of a man.

Poetry, above all things, is a beautiful painting whose tints, to

minute inspection, are confusion worse confounded, but start boldly out to the cursory glance of the connoisseur.

We see an instance of Coleridge's liability to err in his Biographia Literaria—professedly his literary life and opinions, but, in fact, a treatise *de omni scibili et quibusdam aliis.* He goes wrong by reason of his very profundity, and of his error we have a natural type in the contemplation of a star. He who regards it directly and intensely sees, it is true, the star, but it is the star without a ray—while he who surveys it less inquisitively is conscious of all for which the star is useful to us below—its brilliancy and its beauty.

*   *   *

As to Wordsworth, I have no faith in him. That he had, in youth, the feelings of a poet, I believe—for there are glimpses of extreme delicacy in his writings—(and delicacy is the poet's own kingdom—his El Dorado)—but they have the appearance of a better day recollected; and glimpses, at best, are little evidence of present poetic fire—we know that a few straggling flowers spring up daily in the crevices of the Avalanche.

He was to blame in wearing away his youth in contemplation with the end of poetizing in his manhood. With the increase of his judgment the light which should make it apparent has faded away. His judgment consequently is too correct. This may not be understood, but the old Goths of Germany would have understood it, who used to debate matters of importance to their State twice, once when drunk, and once when sober—sober that they might not be deficient in formality—drunk lest they should be destitute of vigor.

The long wordy discussions by which he tries to reason us into admiration of his poetry, speak very little in his favor: they are full of such assertions as this—(I have opened one of his volumes at random) "Of genius the only proof is the act of doing well what is worthy to be done, and what was never done before"—indeed! then it follows that in doing what is unworthy to be done, or what has been done before, no genius can be evinced: yet the picking of pockets is an unworthy

act, pockets have been picked time immemorial, and Barrington, the pick-pocket, in point of genius, would have thought hard of a comparison with William Wordsworth, the poet.

Again—in estimating the merit of certain poems, whether they be Ossian's or M'Pherson's, can surely be of little consequence, yet, in order to prove their worthlessness, Mr. W. has expended many pages in the controversy. *Tantoene animis?* Can great minds descend to such absurdity? But worse still: that he may bear down every argument in favor of these poems, he triumphantly drags forward a passage in his abomination of which he expects the reader to sympathize. It is the beginning of the epic poem "Temora." "The blue waves of Ullin roll in light; the green hills are covered with day; trees shake their dusky heads in the breeze." And this—this gorgeous, yet simple imagery—where all is alive and panting with immortality—than which earth has nothing more grand, nor paradise more beautiful—this—William Wordsworth, the author of Peter Bell, has selected to dignify with his imperial contempt. We shall see what better he, in his own person, has to offer. Imprimis:

> *"And now she's at the poney's head,*
> *And now she's at the poney's tail,*
> *On that side now, and now on this,*
> *And almost stifled her with bliss—*
> *A few sad tears does Betty shed,*
> *She pats the poney where or when*
> *She know not: happy Betty Foy!*
> *O Johnny! never mind the Doctor!"*

Secondly:

> *"The dew was falling fast, the—stars began to blink,*
> *I heard a voice, it said—drink, pretty creature, drink;*
> *And looking o'er the hedge, be—fore me I espied*
> *A snow-white mountain lamb with a—maiden at its side.*

No other sheep were near, the lamb was all alone,
And by a slender cord was—tether'd to a stone."

Now we have no doubt this is all true; we will believe it, indeed we will, Mr. W. Is it sympathy for the sheep you wish to excite? I love a sheep from the bottom of my heart.

*   *   *

But there are occasions, dear B———, there are occasions when Wordsworth is reasonable. Even Stamboul, it is said, shall have an end, and the most unlucky blunders must come to a conclusion. Here is an extract from his preface.

"Those who have been accustomed to the phraseology of modern writers, if they persist in reading this book to a conclusion (impossible!) will, no doubt, have to struggle with feelings of awkwardness; (ha! ha! ha!) they will look round for poetry (ha! ha! ha! ha!) and will be induced to inquire by what species of courtesy these attempts have been permitted to assume that title." Ha! ha! ha! ha! ha!

Yet let not Mr. W. despair; he has given immortality to a wagon, and the bee Sophocles has eternalized a sore toe, and dignified a tragedy with a chorus of turkeys.

*   *   *

Of Coleridge I cannot speak but with reverence. His towering intellect! his gigantic power! To use an author quoted by himself, "J'ai trouvé souvent que la plupart des sectes ont raison dans une bonne partie de ce quelles avànçent, mais non pas en ce quelles nient," and, to employ his own language, he has imprisoned his own conceptions by the barrier he has erected against those of others. It is lamentable to think that such a mind should be buried in metaphysics, and like the Nyctanthes, waste its perfume upon the night alone. In reading that man's poetry I tremble, like one who stands upon a volcano, concious, from the very darkness bursting from the crater, of the fire and the light that are weltering below.

*   *   *

What is Poetry? Poetry! that Proteus-like idea, with as many appellations as the nine-titled Corcyra: Give me, I demanded of a scholar some time ago, give me a definition of poetry? "Très volontiers,"—and he proceeded to his library, brought me a Dr. Johnson, and overwhelmed me with a definition. Shade of the immortal Shakespeare! I imagined to myself the scowl of your spiritual eye upon the profanity of that scurrilous Ursa Major. Think of poetry, dear B———, think of poetry, and then think of—Dr. Samuel Johnson! Think of all that is airy and fairy-like, and then of all that is hideous and unwieldy; think of his huge bulk, the Elephant! and then—and then think of the Tempest—the Midsummer Night's Dream—Prospero—Oberon—and Titania!

*   *   *

A poem, in my opinion, is opposed to a work of science by having, for its *immediate* object, pleasure, not truth; to romance, by having for its object an *indefinite* instead of a *definite* pleasure, being a poem only so far as this object is attained: romance presenting perceptible images with definite, poetry with indefinite sensations, to which end music is an essential, since the comprehension of sweet sound is our most indefinite conception. Music, when combined with a pleasurable idea, is poetry; music without the idea is simply music; the idea without the music is prose from its very definitiveness.

What was meant by the invective against "him who had no music in his soul"?

*   *   *

To sum up this long rigmarole, I have, dear B———, what you no doubt perceive, for the metaphysical poets, as poets, the most sovereign contempt. That they have followers proves nothing—

> *No Indian prince has to his palace*
> *More followers than a thief to the gallows.*

THE PHILOSOPHY OF COMPOSITION

Charles Dickens, in a note now lying before me, alluding to an examination I once made of the mechanism of "Barnaby Rudge," says—"By the way, are you aware that Godwin wrote his 'Caleb Williams' backwards? He first involved his hero in a web of difficulties, forming the second volume, and then, for the first, cast about him for some mode of accounting for what had been done."

I cannot think this the precise mode of procedure on the part of Godwin—and indeed what he himself acknowledges, is not altogether in accordance with Mr. Dickens' idea—but the author of "Caleb Williams" was too good an artist not to perceive the advantage derivable from at least a somewhat similar process. Nothing is more clear than that every plot, worth the name, must be elaborated to its denouement before anything be attempted with the pen. It is only with the denouement constantly in view that we can give a plot its indispensable air of consequence, or causation, by making the incidents, and especially the tone at all points, tend to the development of the intention.

There is a radical error, I think, in the usual mode of constructing a story. Either history affords a thesis—or one is suggested by an incident of the day—or, at best, the author sets himself to work in the combination of striking events to form merely the basis of his narrative—designing, generally, to fill in with description, dialogue, or authorial comment, whatever crevices of fact, or action, may from page to page, render themselves apparent.

I prefer commencing with the consideration of an effect. Keeping originality always in view—for he is false to himself who ventures to dispense with so obvious and so easily attainable a source of interest—I say to myself, in the first place, "Of the innumerable effects, or impressions, of which the heart, the intellect, or (more generally) the soul is susceptible, what one shall I, on the present occasion, select?" Having chosen a novel, first, and secondly a vivid effect, I consider whether it

can be best wrought by incident or tone—whether by ordinary incidents and peculiar tone, or the converse, or by peculiarity both of incident and tone—afterwards looking about me (or rather within) for such combinations of event, or tone, as shall best aid me in the construction of the effect.

I have often thought how interesting a magazine paper might be written by any author who would—that is to say who could—detail, step by step, the processes by which any one of his compositions attained its ultimate point of completion. Why such a paper has never been given to the world, I am much at a loss to say—but, perhaps, the authorial vanity has had more to do with the omission than any one other cause. Most writers—poets in especial—prefer having it understood that they compose by a species of fine frenzy—an ecstatic intuition—and would positively shudder at letting the public take a peep behind the scenes, at the elaborate and vacillating crudities of thought—at the true purposes seized only at the last moment—at the innumerable glimpses of idea that arrived not at the maturity of full view—at the fully matured fancies discarded in despair as unmanageable—at the cautious selections and rejections—at the painful erasures and interpolations—in a word, at the wheels and pinions—the tackle for scene-shifting—the step-ladders and demon-traps—the cock's feathers, the red paint and the black patches, which in ninety-nine cases out of the hundred, constitute the properties of the literary histrio.

I am aware, on the other hand, that the case is by no means common, in which an author is at all in condition to retrace the steps by which his conclusions have been attained. In general, suggestions, having arisen pell-mell, are pursued and forgotten in a similar manner.

For my own part, I have neither sympathy with the repugnance alluded to, nor, at any time the least difficulty in recalling to mind the progressive steps of any of my compositions; and, since the interest of an analysis, or reconstruction, such as I have considered a desideratum, is quite independent of any real or fancied interest in the thing analyzed, it will not be regarded as a breach of decorum on my part to show the *modus operandi* by which some one of my own works was put together.

I select "The Raven," as most generally known. It is my design to render it manifest that no one point in its composition is referable either to accident or intuition—that the work proceeded, step by step, to its completion with the precision and rigid consequence of a mathematical problem.

Let us dismiss, as irrelevant to the poem, *per se,* the circumstance—or say the necessity—which, in the first place, gave rise to the intention of composing a poem that should suit at once the popular and the critical taste.

We commence, then, with this intention.

The initial consideration was that of extent. If any literary work is too long to be read at one sitting, we must be content to dispense with the immensely important effect derivable from unity of impression—for, if two sittings be required, the affairs of the world interfere, and every thing like totality is at once destroyed. But since, *ceteris paribus,* no poet can afford to dispense with any thing that may advance his design, it but remains to be seen whether there is, in extent, any advantage to counterbalance the loss of unity which attends it. Here I say no, at once. What we term a long poem is, in fact, merely a succession of brief ones—that is to say, of brief poetical effects. It is needless to demonstrate that a poem is such, only inasmuch as it intensely excites, by elevating, the soul; and all intense excitements are, through a psychal necessity, brief. For this reason, at least one half of the "Paradise Lost" is essentially prose—a succession of poetical excitements interspersed, inevitably, with corresponding depressions—the whole being deprived, through the extremeness of its length, of the vastly important artistic element, totality, or unity, of effect.

It appears evident, then, that there is a distinct limit, as regards length, to all works of literary art—the limit of a single sitting—and that, although in certain classes of prose composition, such as "Robinson Crusoe," (demanding no unity,) this limit may be advantageously overpassed, it can never properly be overpassed in a poem. Within this limit, the extent of a poem may be made to bear mathematical relation to its merit—in other words, to the excitement or elevation—again in

other words, to the degree of the true poetical effect which it is capable of inducing; for it is clear that the brevity must be in direct ratio of the intensity of the intended effect:—this, with one proviso—that a certain degree of duration is absolutely requisite for the production of any effect at all.

Holding in view these considerations, as well as that degree of excitement which I deemed not above the popular, while not below the critical, taste, I reached at once what I conceived the proper length for my intended poem—a length of about one hundred lines. It is, in fact, a hundred and eight.

My next thought concerned the choice of an impression, or effect, to be conveyed; and here I may as well observe that, throughout the construction, I kept steadily in view the design of rendering the work universally appreciable. I should be carried too far out of my immediate topic were I to demonstrate a point upon which I have repeatedly insisted, and which, with the poetical, stands not in the slightest need of demonstration—the point, I mean, that Beauty is the sole legitimate province of the poem. A few words, however, in elucidation of my real meaning, which some of my friends have evinced a disposition to misrepresent. That pleasure which is at once the most intense, the most elevating, and the most pure, is, I believe, found in the contemplation of the beautiful. When, indeed, men speak of Beauty, they mean, precisely, not a quality, as is supposed, but an effect—they refer, in short, just to that intense and pure elevation of soul—not of intellect, or of heart—upon which I have commented, and which is experienced in consequence of contemplating "the beautiful." Now I designate Beauty as the province of the poem, merely because it is an obvious rule of Art that effects should be made to spring from direct causes—that objects should be attained through means best adapted for their attainment—no one as yet having been weak enough to deny that the peculiar elevation alluded to is most readily attained in the poem. Now the object Truth, or the satisfaction of the intellect, and the object Passion, or the excitement of the heart, are, although attainable, to a certain extent, in poetry, far more readily attainable in prose. Truth, in fact,

demands a precision, and Passion a homeliness (the truly passionate will comprehend me) which are absolutely antagonistic to that Beauty which, I maintain, is the excitement, or pleasurable elevation, of the soul. It by no means follows from any thing here said, that passion, or even truth, may not be introduced, and even profitably introduced, into a poem—for they serve in elucidation, or aid the general effect, as do discords in music, by contrast—but the true artist will always contrive, first, to tone them into proper subservience to the predominant aim, and secondly, to enveil them, as far as possible, in that Beauty which is the atmosphere and the essence of the poem.

Regarding, then, Beauty as my province, my next question referred to the tone of its highest manifestation—and all experience has shown that this tone is one of sadness. Beauty of whatever kind, in its supreme development, invariably excites the sensitive soul to tears. Melancholy is thus the most legitimate of all the poetical tones.

The length, the province, and the tone, being thus determined, I betook myself to ordinary induction, with the view of obtaining some artistic piquancy which might serve me as a key-note in the construction of the poem—some pivot upon which the whole structure might turn. In carefully thinking over all the usual artistic effects—or more properly points, in the theatrical sense—I did not fail to perceive immediately that no one had been so universally employed as that of the refrain. The universality of its employment sufficed to assure me of its intrinsic value, and spared me the necessity of submitting it to analysis. I considered it, however, with regard to its susceptibility of improvement, and soon saw it to be in a primitive condition. As commonly used, the refrain, or burden, not only is limited to lyric verse, but depends for its impression upon the force of monotone—both in sound and thought. The pleasure is deduced solely from the sense of identity—of repetition. I resolved to diversify, and so heighten, the effect, by adhering, in general, to the monotone of sound, while I continually varied that of thought: that is to say, I determined to produce continuously novel effects, by the variation of the application of the refrain—the refrain itself remaining, for the most part, unvaried.

These points being settled, I next bethought me of the nature of my refrain. Since its application was to be repeatedly varied, it was clear that the refrain itself must be brief, for there would have been an insurmountable difficulty in frequent variations of application in any sentence of length. In proportion to the brevity of the sentence, would, of course, be the facility of the variation. This led me at once to a single word as the best refrain.

The question now arose as to the character of the word. Having made up my mind to a refrain, the division of the poem into stanzas was, of course, a corollary: the refrain forming the close of each stanza. That such a close, to have force, must be sonorous and susceptible of protracted emphasis, admitted no doubt: and these considerations inevitably led me to the long *o* as the most sonorous vowel, in connection with *r* as the most producible consonant.

The sound of the refrain being thus determined, it became necessary to select a word embodying this sound, and at the same time in the fullest possible keeping with that melancholy which I had predetermined as the tone of the poem. In such a search it would have been absolutely impossible to overlook the word "Nevermore." In fact, it was the very first which presented itself.

The next desideratum was a pretext for the continuous use of the one word "nevermore." In observing the difficulty which I at once found in inventing a sufficiently plausible reason for its continuous repetition, I did not fail to perceive that this difficulty arose solely from the pre-assumption that the word was to be so continuously or monotonously spoken by a human being—I did not fail to perceive, in short, that the difficulty lay in the reconciliation of this monotony with the exercise of reason on the part of the creature repeating the word. Here, then, immediately arose the idea of a non-reasoning creature capable of speech; and, very naturally, a parrot, in the first instance, suggested itself, but was superseded forthwith by a Raven, as equally capable of speech, and infinitely more in keeping with the intended tone.

I had now gone so far as the conception of a Raven—the bird of ill omen—monotonously repeating the one word, "Nevermore," at the

conclusion of each stanza, in a poem of melancholy tone, and in length about one hundred lines. Now, never losing sight of the object supremeness, or perfection, at all points, I asked myself—"Of all melancholy topics, what, according to the universal understanding of mankind, is the most melancholy?" Death—was the obvious reply. "And when," I said, "is this most melancholy of topics most poetical?" From what I have already explained at some length, the answer, here also, is obvious—"When it most closely allies itself to Beauty: the death, then, of a beautiful woman is, unquestionably, the most poetical topic in the world—and equally is it beyond doubt that the lips best suited for such topic are those of a bereaved lover."

I had now to combine the two ideas, of a lover lamenting his deceased mistress and a Raven continuously repeating the word "Nevermore."—I had to combine these, bearing in mind my design of varying, at every turn, the application of the word repeated; but the only intelligible mode of such combination is that of imagining the Raven employing the word in answer to the queries of the lover. And here it was that I saw at once the opportunity afforded for the effect on which I had been depending—that is to say, the effect of the variation of application. I saw that I could make the first query propounded by the lover—the first query to which the Raven should reply "Nevermore"—that I could make this first query a commonplace one—the second less so—the third still less, and so on—until at length the lover, startled from his original nonchalance by the melancholy character of the word itself—by its frequent repetition—and by a consideration of the ominous reputation of the fowl that uttered it—is at length excited to superstition, and wildly propounds queries of a far different character—queries whose solution he has passionately at heart—propounds them half in superstition and half in that species of despair which delights in self-torture—propounds them not altogether because he believes in the prophetic or demoniac character of the bird (which, reason assures him, is merely repeating a lesson learned by rote) but because he experiences a phrenzied pleasure in so modeling his questions as to receive from the expected "Nevermore" the most delicious because

the most intolerable of sorrow. Perceiving the opportunity thus afforded me—or, more strictly, thus forced upon me in the progress of the construction—I first established in mind the climax, or concluding query—that query to which "Nevermore" should be in the last place an answer—that in reply to which this word "Nevermore" should involve the utmost conceivable amount of sorrow and despair.

Here then the poem may be said to have its beginning—at the end, where all works of art should begin—for it was here, at this point of my preconsiderations, that I first put pen to paper in the composition of the stanza:

> *"Prophet," said I, "thing of evil!—prophet still, if bird*
> *or devil!*
> *By that Heaven that bends above us—by that God we*
> *both adore—*
> *Tell this soul with sorrow laden, if, within the distant*
> *Aidenn,*
> *It shall clasp a sainted maiden whom the angels name*
> *Lenore—*
> *Clasp a rare and radiant maiden whom the angels name*
> *Lenore."*
>
> *Quoth the Raven "Nevermore."*

I composed this stanza, at this point, first that, by establishing the climax, I might the better vary and graduate, as regards seriousness and importance, the preceding queries of the lover—and, secondly, that I might definitely settle the rhythm, the metre, and the length and general arrangement of the stanza—as well as graduate the stanzas which were to precede, so that none of them might surpass this in rhythmical effect. Had I been able, in the subsequent composition, to construct more vigorous stanzas, I should, without scruple, have purposely enfeebled them, so as not to interfere with the climacteric effect.

And here I may as well say a few words of the versification. My first object (as usual) was originality. The extent to which this has been

neglected, in versification, is one of the most unaccountable things in the world. Admitting that there is little possibility of variety in mere rhythm, it is still clear that the possible varieties of metre and stanza are absolutely infinite—and yet, for centuries, no man, in verse, has ever done, or ever seemed to think of doing, an original thing. The fact is, that originality (unless in minds of very unusual force) is by no means a matter, as some suppose, of impulse or intuition. In general, to be found, it must be elaborately sought, and although a positive merit of the highest class, demands in its attainment less of invention than negation.

Of course, I pretend to no originality in either the rhythm or metre of the "Raven." The former is trochaic—the latter is octameter acatalectic, alternating with heptameter catalectic repeated in the refrain of the fifth verse, and terminating with tetrameter catalectic. Less pedantically—the feet employed throughout (trochees) consist of a long syllable followed by a short: the first line of the stanza consists of eight of these feet—the second of seven and a half (in effect two-thirds)—the third of eight—the fourth of seven and a half—the fifth the same—the sixth three and a half. Now, each of these lines, taken individually, has been employed before, and what originality the "Raven" has, is in their combination into stanza; nothing even remotely approaching this combination has ever been attempted. The effect of this originality of combination is aided by other unusual, and some altogether novel effects, arising from an extension of the application of the principles of rhyme and alliteration.

The next point to be considered was the mode of bringing together the lover and the Raven—and the first branch of this consideration was the locale. For this the most natural suggestion might seem to be a forest, or the fields—but it has always appeared to me that a close circumscription of space is absolutely necessary to the effect of insulated incident:—it has the force of a frame to a picture. It has an indisputable moral power in keeping concentrated the attention, and, of course, must not be confounded with mere unity of place.

I determined, then, to place the lover in his chamber—in a cham-

ber rendered sacred to him by memories of her who had frequented it. The room is represented as richly furnished—this is mere pursuance of the ideas I have already explained on the subject of Beauty, as the sole true poetical thesis.

The locale being thus determined, I had now to introduce the bird—and the thought of introducing him through the window, was inevitable. The idea of making the lover suppose, in the first instance, that the flapping of the wings of the bird against the shutter, is a "tapping" at the door, originated in a wish to increase, by prolonging the reader's curiosity, and in a desire to admit the incidental effect arising from the lover's throwing open the door, finding all dark, and thence adopting the half-fancy that it was the spirit of his mistress that knocked.

I made the night tempestuous, first, to account for the Raven's seeking admission, and secondly, for the effect of contrast with the (physical) serenity within the chamber.

I made the bird alight on the bust of Pallas, also for the effect of contrast between the marble and the plumage—it being understood that the bust was absolutely suggested by the bird—the bust of Pallas being chosen, first, as most in keeping with the scholarship of the lover, and, secondly, for the sonorousness of the word, Pallas, itself.

About the middle of the poem, also, I have availed myself of the force of contrast, with a view of deepening the ultimate impression. For example, an air of the fantastic—approaching as nearly to the ludicrous as was admissible—is given to the Raven's entrance. He comes in "with many a flirt and flutter."

> *Not the least obeisance made he; not a moment stopped or stayed he;*
> *But, with mien of lord or lady, perched above my chamber door—*

In the two stanzas which follow, the design is more obviously carried out:—

> *Then this ebony bird beguiling my sad fancy into smiling,*
> *By the grave and stern decorum of the countenance it wore,*

> "Though thy crest be shorn and shaven, thou," I said, "art sure no
> craven,
> Ghastly grim and ancient Raven wandering from the Nightly shore—
> Tell me what thy lordly name is on the Night's Plutonian shore?"
>> Quoth the Raven, "Nevermore."
>
> Much I marvelled this ungainly fowl to hear discourse so plainly,
> Though its answer little meaning—little relevancy bore;
> For we cannot help agreeing that no living human being
> Ever yet was blessed with seeing bird above his chamber door—
> Bird or beast upon the sculptured bust above his chamber door,
>> With such a name as "Nevermore."

The effect of the denouement being thus provided for, I immediately drop the fantastic for a tone of the most profound seriousness:—this tone commencing in the stanza directly following the one last quoted, with the line,

> But the Raven, sitting lonely on that placid bust, spoke only, etc.

From this epoch the lover no longer jests—no longer sees any thing even of the fantastic in the Raven's demeanor. He speaks of him as a "grim, ungainly, ghastly, gaunt, and ominous bird of yore," and feels the "fiery eyes" burning into his "bosom's core." This revolution of thought, or fancy, on the lover's part, is intended to induce a similar one on the part of the reader—to bring the mind into a proper frame for the denouement—which is now brought about as rapidly and as directly as possible.

With the denouement proper—with the Raven's reply, "Nevermore," to the lover's final demand if he shall meet his mistress in another world—the poem, in its obvious phase, that of a simple narrative, may be said to have its completion. So far, every thing is within the limits of the accountable—of the real. A raven, having learned by rote the single word "Nevermore," and having escaped from the custody of its owner, is driven at midnight, through the violence of a storm, to seek

admission at a window from which a light still gleams—the chamber-window of a student, occupied half in poring over a volume, half in dreaming of a beloved mistress deceased. The casement being thrown open at the fluttering of the bird's wings, the bird itself perches on the most convenient seat out of the immediate reach of the student, who, amused by the incident and the oddity of the visitor's demeanor, demands of it, in jest and without looking for a reply, its name. The raven addressed, answers with its customary word, "Nevermore"—a word which finds immediate echo in the melancholy heart of the student, who, giving utterance aloud to certain thoughts suggested by the occasion, is again startled by the fowl's repetition of "Nevermore." The student now guesses the state of the case, but is impelled, as I have before explained, by the human thirst for self-torture, and in part by superstition, to propound such queries to the bird as will bring him, the lover, the most of the luxury of sorrow, through the anticipated answer, "Nevermore." With the indulgence, to the extreme, of this self-torture, the narration, in which I have termed its first or obvious phase, has a natural termination, and so far there has been no overstepping of the limits of the real.

But in subjects so handled, however skilfully, or with however vivid an array of incident, there is always a certain hardness or nakedness, which repels the artistical eye. Two things are invariably required—first, some amount of complexity, or more properly, adaptation; and, secondly, some amount of suggestiveness—some under-current, however indefinite, of meaning. It is this latter, in especial, which imparts to a work of art so much of that richness (to borrow from colloquy a forcible term) which we are too fond of confounding with the ideal. It is the excess of the suggested meaning—it is the rendering this the upper instead of the under-current of the theme—which turns into prose (and that of the very flattest kind) the so called poetry of the so called transcendentalists.

Holding these opinions, I added the two concluding stanzas of the poem—their suggestiveness being thus made to pervade all the narrative which has preceded them. The under-current of meaning is rendered first apparent in the lines—

> *"Take thy beak from out my heart, and take thy form from off my door!"*
> *Quoth the Raven, "Nevermore!"*

It will be observed that the words, "from out my heart," involve the first metaphorical expression in the poem. They, with the answer, "Nevermore," dispose the mind to seek a moral in all that has been previously narrated. The reader begins now to regard the Raven as emblematical—but it is not until the very last line of the very last stanza, that the intention of making him emblematical of Mournful and Never-ending Remembrance is permitted distinctly to be seen:

> *And the Raven, never flitting, still is sitting, still is sitting*
> *On the pallid bust of Pallas just above my chamber door;*
> *And his eyes have all the seeming of a demon's that is dreaming,*
> *And the lamp-light o'er him streaming throws his shadow on the floor;*
> *And my soul from out that shadow that lies floating on the floor*
> *   Shall be lifted—nevermore!*

NOTES

The Lake

Mabbott says this is Lake Drummond, located 100 miles southeast of Richmond in Virginia's Great Dismal Swamp, about which, in 1803, Thomas Moore wrote "A Ballad: The Lake of the Dismal Swamp." Nothing in Poe's poem definitely links it to Lake Drummond.

Sonnet—To Science

Richard Wilbur writes "it may be read as a standard romantic protest against Cartesian dualism, against the exclusion of value from the world of fact."

To The River Po

Poe doubtless intended to pun on his name with the title of this conventionally emblematic poem. Nevertheless, north of Richmond the Po River flows, becoming part of the Mattaponi.

Fairy-Land

Poe saw the poem's character as "archness . . . which is unfailingly poetic" and meant fantasy as well as humor.

Alone

Found in Baltimore in 1875, without title, "Alone" was thought to be a forgery, but Prof. I.B. Cauthen and others proved it is Poe's.

To Helen

Although the poem was first published in 1831, lines 9–10 were not added until 1843. Poe said in 1848 that he had written the poem "to the first, purely ideal love of my soul." This was Mrs. Jane Stith Stanard, who died insane in Poe's fifteenth year. Helen of Troy is the symbol of classical beauty. The word "Nicean," its reference arguable, seems to mean "the victors." Naiads are nymphs or water spirits.

Israfel

Israfel is an angel who represents an ideal other world.

The Sleeper

Originally published as "Irene" (Greek for Peace). The poem's "sleeper" is a dead woman. Poe once said that he thought the poem better than "The Raven." Lethe is the mythic river of the dead.

To One In Paradise

Poe based his poem on a story concerning Byron and his young love, Mary Chaworth. He had written of this story in the December 1844 issue of the *Columbian Magazine*.

The Coliseum

Poe's referent is the Roman coliseum. He submitted this poem and a story, "MS. Found in a Bottle," to a contest sponsored by the *Baltimore Saturday Visiter*. Winning the fifty dollar fiction prize, he said he won the poetry prize as well but it was taken from him. This marks Poe's literary emergence. The blank verse is unusual for Poe.

Bridal Ballad

A. H. Quinn notes that this is Poe's only poem spoken by a woman. Allen Tate thought Poe might have imagined this to be the voice of

Elmira Royster Shelton when she discovered that her father had intercepted Poe's letters, causing her to marry the wrong man.

The Haunted Palace

Poe's palace is an allegory of a man's head. He once argued that Longfellow plagiarized this poem. "Porphyrogene" means to Poe "born to the purple" or royalty.

The Conqueror Worm

Wilbur says "The universe has reached maximum diffusion and incoherence, the Earth is physically and spiritually at its remotest from God (hence 'lonesome'), and its purgation by cataclysm is at hand."

Lenore

Part of a burial service, "Peccavimus" means "we have sinned."

Dream-Land

An "eidolon" is a phantom. The "ultimate dim Thule" refers to a very distant island, apparently barren, as a place of exile.

Eulalie—A Song

Dwight Macdonald thought the poem so bad he anthologized it in *Parodies From Chaucer to Beerbohm.* If "The Raven" is Poe at his darkest, "Eulalie" may be his most ebullient moment.

The Raven

The most dramatically staged of Poe's poems, this allegory of contact with the world beyond death is deeply flawed yet remains central in Poe's work. Auden thought its form and theme in endless conflict. So powerful is its appeal, however, that the image of the raven is enough to evoke Poe's name and poetry. Readers interested in sources can

consult Thomas Ollive Mabbott's *The Poems of Edgar Allan Poe.* Poe offered the poem to *Graham's Magazine,* in New York, and it was rejected, then purchased for fifteen dollars and published by the *American Review* of February 1845—but under the nom de plume of "Quarles." However, the New York *Evening Mirror* had secured the right to reprint the poem, and its "reprint" came out before the binding of the *American Review.* Thus, the poem actually appeared January 29, 1845 for the first time, and under Poe's name.

A Valentine to——————

The name of Poe's friend, Frances Sargeant Osgood, is spelled by the first letter of the first line, the second letter of the second line, etc. A "Gordian knot" is an extreme difficulty. Ferdinand Mendez Pinto was a sixteenth-century Portuguese author famed as a liar.

Ulalume—A Ballad

Poe's ghost story plot is based on Elizabeth Oakes Smith's "The Summons Answered" of 1844. "Ulalume" is a female name for light. Auber probably refers to Daniel-Francois-Esprit Auber, the composer, and Weir probably is Robert Walter Weir, a painter of the Hudson River School. Allen Tate thought both names were made up.

The Bells

Marie Louise Shew Houghton, in 1875, recalled that Poe visited her in New York, complaining he had to write a poem but had no subject or inspiration. She then started, in Poe's style, a poem called "The Bells"— because bells were ringing outside. Whether they were fire bells or church bells is unknown. Poe finished the poem, sold it for fifteen dollars to *Union Magazine,* then revised and sold it to *Sartain's Union Magazine* for forty-five dollars. It is often anthologized to show sonic techniques (onomatopoeia, assonance, consonance).

To Helen

Mrs. Sarah Helen Whitman, of Providence, was a widow and poet to whom Poe was engaged after the death of his wife. He promised not to drink and when he broke the promise she broke the engagement.

For Annie

While Poe courted Mrs. Whitman, he wooed Mrs. Nancy Locke Heywood Richmond of Lowell, Massachusetts. Theirs was, as he said, a "Platonic" relationship, but his letters to her are desperately loving. Having left her on the night of November 16, 1848, he was distraught enough to attempt suicide. He wrote "I swallowed about half the laudanum. . . . A friend was at hand, who . . . saved me." Poe's name for Mrs. Richmond was "Annie." After his death she made it legally her own. "To Annie" is, Wilbur says, "a direct statement of Poe's Oedipal feelings, of his horror of the physical and his consequent devotion to fantasies of spiritual union in death."

Eldorado

"Eldorado" reflects the California gold rush and American fever to grow rich. The word names a symbolic land of promise.

To My Mother

"Mother" here is Poe's aunt and mother-in-law, Maria Clemm, whom he called "Muddy." Virginia was Poe's wife and Mrs. Clemm's daughter.

Annabel Lee

Numerous women have been advanced as the inspiration for "Annabel Lee." The most likely candidate seems to be Mrs. "Annie" Richmond, who received the poem from Poe's hand, but this is unprovable.

Letter to B—

Published as the preface to *Poems* of 1831 and reprinted in the *Southern Literary Messenger* in 1836, the "Letter" is thought to have been addressed to Elam Bliss, the publisher of the *Poems*.

The Philosophy of Composition

For a discussion of this essay, readers might consider Daniel Hoffman's "The Rationale of Verse" in his *Poe Poe Poe Poe Poe Poe Poe* (Doubleday, 1972).

ABOUT THE EDITOR

Dave Smith is professor of American literature and creative writing at Louisiana State University in Baton Rouge, Louisiana. The most recent of his books of poetry are The Roundhouse Voices: Selected and New Poems *and* Cuba Night. *He is the editor of* The Pure Clear Word: Essays On the Poetry of James Wright *and has edited, with David Bottoms,* The Morrow Anthology of Younger American Poets. *He is also the author of a novel,* Onliness, *and a collection of critical essays,* Local Assays: On Contemporary American Poetry.